Lafayette in Transnational Context

Lafayette in Transnational Context:

Identity, Travel, and Nationalism in the Revolutionary Atlantic World

Edited by
Jordan Kellman

University of Louisiana at Lafayette Press
2015

Portions of "Lafayette's Historical Legacy: Politics, Culture, and the Modern World" first appeared in Anne C. Loveland, *Emblem of Liberty: The Image of Lafayette in the American Mind* (Baton Rouge: LSU Press, 1971); it is reprinted here with the permission of the publisher.

ISBN 13 (paper): 978-1-935754-67-1

http://ulpress.org
University of Louisiana at Lafayette Press
P.O. Box 40831
Lafayette, LA 70504-0831

Printed on acid-free paper.

Library of Congress Cataloging-in-Publication Data

Lafayette in transnational context : identity, travel, and nationalism in the Revolutionary Atlantic world / edited by Jordan Kellman.
pages cm
ISBN 978-1-935754-67-1
1. Lafayette, Marie Joseph Paul Yves Roch Gilbert Du Motier, marquis de, 1757-1834. 2. Lafayette, Marie Joseph Paul Yves Roch Gilbert Du Motier, marquis de, 1757-1834--Travel--United States. 3. United States--History--Revolution, 1775-1783--Participation, French. 4. France--History--Revolution, 1789-1799. I. Kellman, Jordan, 1966- editor.
E207.L2L34 2015
973.3'24--dc23

2015016621

To the memory of Bradley Pollock

Contents

Acknowledgments

This book would not have been possible without the help and encouragement of many people and organizations. First, I thank the Lafayette Consolidated Government's Marquis de Lafayette Committee and the University of Louisiana at Lafayette's History Department for the financial support that made this project possible. Philippe Gustin, Director of the Centre International de Lafayette, and Lynne Durel, Chair of the Marquis de Lafayette Committee, provided crucial encouragement and support from the beginning. At the University of Louisiana at Lafayette, David Barry, then Dean of Liberal Arts and Robert Carriker, Head of the History department helped in countless ways. Michael Martin, Director of the University's Center for Louisiana Studies, and James Wilson at the UL Lafayette Press provided encouragement at every stage and worked tirelessly to see this collection through publication. Special thanks are due to the contributors, whose insights, goodwill, and patience have been crucial to the collection's success. Finally, I would like to thank my family, Maribel Dietz, Francisco and Gisèle Kellman for their patience and inspiration throughout this project.

Introduction

This volume represents a reappraisal of the life, career, accomplishments, experience, and impact of a singular figure in French and American History, one who has been well-known enough for long enough to have his own historiography. The broad outlines of that historiography are evident: First lauded as a lynchpin of the American Revolution, the Marquis de Lafayette is credited with both personally aiding the American struggle for independence and securing the support of France at crucial intervals during the American War for Independence. He discovered a passion for the American cause at a young age and directed his considerable influence and resources towards its success throughout his life. And yet doubts remained about his legacy. His famous inability to bring the same success to the French Revolution, and to successfully cross social and cultural boundaries, effectively led to both his own imprisonment and his failure to steer the Revolution in the direction that he envisioned.

The essays in this collection stem from the celebration in Lafayette, Louisiana, of the 250th anniversary of Lafayette's birth in 1757. The series aimed to not only provide a communal celebration of this symbol of French-American relations, but also to spark a deep reflection on the historical lessons that Lafayette's life and career offer to a modern multicultural community. An extremely diverse set of participants and audience members from different parts of the civic and scholarly community debated these questions with the passion that comes only from having both true historical and civic engagement.

The essays also represent the intersection of two recent historiographical movements that have changed the landscape of both French and American history writing and our understanding of the meaning and significance of a wide range of historical events and actors. First, the cultural turn in history has seen a new focus on how historical figures such as the Marquis were influenced by cultural norms, expectations, and currents prevalent at the time, and on how these played a decisive role not only in their actions but in how those actions were read and interpreted by contemporaries. Crucially, this focus does not amount to a dismissal of their originality or sincerity: different actors can be placed in the same cultural milieu and act very differently. It does, however, indicate that to achieve a full understanding of historical figures and their impact we must move beyond an examination of their characters and personal circumstances to an understanding of the world in which they lived. In the case of Lafayette, this is a complex task involving the unpacking of the military and economic traditions of early modern French society, as well as the new dynamic of American political culture, race relations, and populism.[1] The thrust of most historical scholarship since the middle of the twentieth century has in fact been to swing to the opposite extreme, emphasizing the historical power of broad social, cultural, linguistic, political, physical, and biological forces rather than the conscious will of extraordinary individuals. To fully understand the figure of Lafayette and his significance to the larger histories of France and the United States, an understanding of both approaches and the many ways in which they are interwoven is necessary, and it is toward that end that these essays collectively aim.

Second, Lafayette occupies a special place in what has come to be known as the Atlantic world. The historical understanding of the societies, nations, and cultures that bordered the Atlantic Ocean has undergone a dramatic reorientation in the past twenty years. Previously, national histories tended to be studied more or less independently of each other and as if the ocean that both separated them and connected them was not there. Historical figures were usually classified as belonging to a single national history and identity, and they were generally studied primarily by specialists of those national histories. A perspective centered on the ocean rather than landmasses, places of contested and multinational interaction rather than sovereign territories, was first suggested by the work of members of the Annales school, notably Ferdinand Braudel, to take account of the tremendous historical significance of oceans and seas on the societies that grew up around them and as historical forces guiding the development of those societies and cultures—forces that had been obscured for centuries as historians focused on the conscious deeds of men and their short-term actions and consequences.[2] Much of the work

1. See Lloyd Kramer, *Lafayette in Two Worlds: Public Cultures and Personal Identities in an Age of Revolutions* (Chapel Hill: University of North Carolina Press, 1996, 2-8.

2. Fernand Braudel, *La Méditerranée et le Monde Méditerranéen a l'époque de Philippe*

of the Annales scholars was focused on the Mediterranean and the Mediterranean world, which left a large area of historical inquiry concerning the Atlantic open to the next generation of historians. At the same time, scholars such as Bernard Baylin were growing frustrated with the limitations of understanding the complex interactions between the new and old Anglophone worlds in the traditional terms of national histories and found the perspective of the ocean, the Atlantic world, to be both liberating and fruitful in uncovering patterns and connections obscured by the nationalist perspective.[3]

Though Atlantic world historiography began with a re-envisioning of the social, political, and economic forces that characterized the Anglophone societies of Britain and the British American colonies and young republic, its essential perspective has now been adopted by historians of the early modern French, Spanish, and African interactions around and across the Atlantic Ocean. In particular, a new generation of scholars of the French colonies has begun to explore how complex interactions in the Francophone Atlantic world played a decisive role in shaping not only the path of Caribbean, Canadian, and American history, but also African and European history.[4] This re-envisioning has produced a new understanding of just how many people operated in an arena bounded not by national borders but by the reach of sailing ships, trade routes, communication, and control from Senegal to La Rochelle to New England to Saint Domingue to Louisiana.[5] These studies have taught us a great deal about the possibilities for self-invention, the mobilization of local knowledge and resources, and the malleability of social norms across these boundaries. This new perspective has also placed the histories of early modern England, France, Spain, Africa, and the Americas squarely in a global context and the realm of global history, which seeks to broaden the focus of inquiry even further in order to decipher global historical patterns.[6] Such phenomena as the rise of democratic institutions and

---

II, 3 vols. (Paris: A. Colin, 1949)

3. See, for example, Bernard Bailyn, *Atlantic History: Concepts and Contours* (Cambridge, Mass., 2005); Silvia Marzagalli, "Sur les origins de l'Atlantic History," *Dix-huitième* siècle 33 (2001): 17-31.

4. See, for example, Jordan Kellman, ed., *Beyond Center and Periphery: new Currents in French and Francophone Atlantic Studies, Atlantic Studies* 10, no. 1 (2013).

5. Bill Marshall, *The French Atlantic: Travels in Culture and History* (Liverpool: Liverpool University Press, 2009).

6. Peter Coclanis, "Atlantic World or Atlantic/World?," *William and Mary Quarterly*, 63:4 (October, 2006), 725-42; Nicholas Canny, "Atlantic History and Global History,"

ideologies, patterns of warfare and economic interaction are here seen as emerging not from any local, national, or even regional traditions, but instead as emerging from the broad matrix of global interactions and influences.[7]

In certain key respects, though, the promise of Atlantic history has not yet been fulfilled. In many ways the national boundaries that it sought to replace have reemerged in the consideration of the Atlantic world itself. While the first wave of Atlantic history was centered around New England and the Anglophone North Atlantic, we now have largely geographically and historiographically separate areas of scholarship of the Francophone Atlantic (encompassing Canada, early Florida, Louisiana, the Antilles, and early French colonies in Brazil) and a Spanish Atlantic (focused on Florida, the Caribbean, Mexico, and South America). A second area in which the fruits of Atlantic History have yet to be fully realized relates to the historical actors whom historians choose to study. These efforts have been extremely successful at expanding the circle of influential figures beyond the traditional cadre of founding fathers and statesmen to a whole host of players who existed on the borders and boundaries of this teeming Atlantic world, exploring the periphery and often taking advantage of their mobility to increase their standing in the metropolitan center.[8] Scholars have been less successful at reconceptualizing and refocusing public attention on the statesmen and heroes who made up the pantheon of eighteenth-century British and revolutionary American history.[9] And yet the insights gained from this approach can be every bit as fruitful in reexamining the lives and legacies of those originally credited with prosecuting the revolutions of the Atlantic.

In so many ways, no figure in Atlantic history is as able to address these rifts and lacunae, and is as ripe for reexamination in the context that Atlantic

---

Jack P. Greene and Philip D. Morgan, *Atlantic History: A Critical Reappraisal* (Oxford: Oxford University Press, 2009), 317-36.

7. *Soundings in Atlantic History: Latent Structures and Intellectual Currents, 1500-1830*, ed. Bernard Bailyn and Patricia Denault (Cambridge, MA: Harvard University Press, 2009), 21-25.

8. P. Linebaugh and M. Rediker, *The Many-Headed Hydra: The Hidden History of the Revolutionary Atlantic* (London: Verso, 2002); For an example, see Neil Safier, "A Courier between Empires: Hipolito da Costa and the Atlantic World," in Bailyn and Denault, *Atlantic History*, 265-93.

9. For an excellent recent contribution to this effort, see François Furstenberg, *In the Name of the Father: Washington's Legacy, Slavery, and the Making of a Nation* (Penguin: 2006).

history provides, as the Marquis de Lafayette. A true creator of the Atlantic world *avant la lettre*, Lafayette has the unusual combination of having played significant roles in an astonishing number of revolutionary events on both sides of the Atlantic. While his family roots run deep in the French military aristocracy, he conceived of his trajectory from a very early age as a transatlantic one.[10] His lifelong struggle to bring the resources of the old world to the new and the insights of the new world to the old—and to bring the social upheaval of the French Revolution and the economic revolution of the Americas and the Caribbean into what he saw as one emergent liberal democratic moral order—drove his every move, battle, and speech.[11] As such, his own life reflects the revolutionary drama that played out across the Atlantic in the eighteenth and early nineteenth centuries, and the emergent historical understanding of the Atlantic world can now serve to illuminate that life and legacy. The essays in this volume all seek to bring these perspectives full circle, examining the many facets of the life and career of the Marquis de Lafayette as they played out in the multivalent, multicultural world within which he lived his life and made his name.

Lloyd Kramer argues persuasively that Lafayette is unique among historical figures because he was directly involved, in both symbolic and highly pragmatic ways, in the major changes that marked the transition to modernity in the eighteenth and early nineteenth centuries. He was a zealous and lifelong exponent and defender of the new concept of human rights and the cause of democratic revolutions and, unlike many other theorists, he fought, suffered, and risked his life repeatedly in the military struggles that sought to defend them, from the Virginia campaign to the Parisian National Guard. He defended the new movement toward nationalism in the cases not only of the United States, but also of Greece, Italy, and Poland. He embodied the Romantic ideal of heroic individual action to intervene in the world based on the pursuit of principle or an ideal vision. He championed the rights of enslaved Africans, and held the independence and intellectual abilities of women in very high esteem, treating both as equals in his interactions. He emphasized the importance of free economic growth and international interaction and exchange as necessary paths to progress, promoting cross-cultural exchange, trans-nationalism, and American-European trade on all his visits.

10. See David A. Clary, *Adopted Son: Washington, Lafayette and the Friendship that Saved the Revolution* (New York: Bantam, 2007), 86-111.

11. Harlow Giles Unger, *Lafayette* (Hoboken: Wiley and Sons, 2002) documents many of these engagements but remains loyal to an antediluvian historiography of unexamined reverence.

Lafayette became a fellow-traveler for transnationals seeking identity in an increasingly fragmented, modern world. Kramer ends with an empassioned plea to revisit the example of Lafayette as an antidote to the cynicism that pervades contemporary discussions of the power of government and political ideas to improve society.

Sandra Frink's essay unravels the dense knot of nationalism, regionalism, ethnic and linguistic identity, and political and military rivalry that characterized New Orleans in the first quarter of the nineteenth century by analyzing Lafayette's visit to the city as part of his 1824 tour of the United States. Frink shows how in New Orleans an unprecedented number of groups vied for attention, place, and primacy in the celebrations surrounding the Marquis's visit. Choctaw Indians, Anglo immigrants, and Creole elites alike sought to use the occasion to settle scores and assert their prominence in New Orleans society. Though Lafayette would seem to be the ideal hero for the Anglo-French city to celebrate, his connections to France made him suspect in the eyes of Anglo leaders bent on controlling and assimilating the city's francophone creole population and power structure. At the same time, his deep connections to the Revolutionary War and its New England theater stoked anxieties among the Creole residents of the Latin-Caribbean port city. Together, these groups sought to overcome pervasive doubts about the extent to which New Orleans could be considered a truly American city and the extent to which New Orleanians, particularly those of French descent and language, could be trusted to represent and defend the fledgling republic. Women were conspicuously absent from the celebrations, victims of an increasingly sexist society bent on displaying its patriarchal military vigor to the general who had helped to secure the nation's liberty. Lafayette's tour of 1824 has been understood as a unifying moment in American history and, in particular, in the formation of a unified American national identity. Frink's essay illuminates not only the limits of the famously unifying power of Lafayette and his tour, but also the deeply fractured nature of the young republic and the tensions that lay just beneath the surface, sometimes erupting even in the celebration of perhaps its most uncontroversial hero.

The central question of Sylvia Neely's article is firmly rooted in the questions raised by the concept of a coherent and interconnected Atlantic world: Why did the Marquis de Lafayette's attempt to import the ideas and successes of the American Revolution fail? Neely's answer does much to undo facile assumptions and historical myths about Lafayette. First, she places his much-criticized thirst for fame and glory in the context of prevalent assumptions in the new republic, especially among figures like George Washington, for whom such a quest was taken to be synonymous with the improvement of humankind generally. This interpretation did not hold in France: during the revolutionary years, when individual leadership was more and more suspect, Lafayette was bitterly criticized as vainglorious. Neely shows that Lafayette's attempts to import the successes of American leadership fell flat, largely due to Louis XVI's personality, but also because of Lafayette's own desire to remain in the background and support an orderly transfer of power rather than seize control himself. Neely develops an understanding of the large but finite credibility and social capital that Lafayette brought back with him to France, and shows how that currency slowly ran out as he was forced to use more and more of it to keep the peace among the revolutionaries, the National Guard, and the populace. Beginning with Louis XVI's famously thwarted attempts to leave Paris for Saint Cloud at Easter in 1791 and the flight to Varenne that summer, and culminating in the Massacre of the Champ de Mars, Lafayette found himself overtaken by events. He was suspected of treachery against the revolutionary movement, a charge that certainly misconstrued his intentions, though as the revolution became more radical his own law-and-order understanding of it was indeed left behind. When the Revolutionary War faltered in 1792, Louis XIV was deposed and Lafayette schemed to have him reinstated: the revolutionaries, including the National Guard, finally turned on the Marquis decisively, declaring him a traitor and an outlaw on the eve of the Reign of Terror. In other words, the forces unleashed by the revolution and freedom from government in France proved too overpowering for the kind of sober, consensus-based progress that Lafayette took as the model from the American Revolution. His authorship of the original draft of the French Declaration of the Rights of Man, much of which survives in the final version, demonstrates the longevity of the concepts Lafayette hoped to bring to France, even if he was not successful at implanting them politically.

Through deep examination of Lafayette's correspondence, Anne Loveland traces both the involvement and the influence of Lafayette on the American response to three foreign revolutions: the French Revolution, the Greek overthrow of Turkish rule, and the July Revolution of 1830. In the case of the French Revolution of 1789, Lafayette's own presence in the early phase of the revolution helped to lead Americans to see it as a natural extension of their own revolution, in which Lafayette had played such a key role. His eventual fall from power, and the plunge from revolution into terror, led Americans to view the uprising as a betrayal of both their own revolution and of the Marquis and his principles. Lafayette tirelessly supported American intervention in the Greek Revolution of 1821-1830, drawing on the stature of classical Greek civilization and its role in the framing of the republic, in an effort to persuade Americans that coming to the aid of Greece was a natural consequence of the arc of history that had created the American republic itself. Loveland argues that it was under Lafayette's influence that a handful of Americans joined the military effort in spite of broad political rejection of American involvement in overseas conflicts. Together, the course of the French and Greek revolutions led Americans to question the suitability for export of the American model of revolution and creation of a democratic republic. Lafayette's assumption of the command of the National Guard in the July Revolution of 1830 gave Americans great confidence and the relatively bloodless prosecution of the revolution reaffirmed their faith in the French path toward democracy, in spite of the fact that a constitutional monarchy resulted with Louis XVI remaining on the throne. Loveland makes clear that many Americans saw these other revolutions as failures to heed the example offered by the United States in all its particulars. These differences caused Americans to probe deeper into what it meant to be American, suggesting for example that widespread landownership, and the potential to attain it, gave Americans a different kind of investment in the well-being of the State. In spite of the perceived failure and compromises of each of these revolutions, Loveland shows that Lafayette himself remained in the eyes of his American correspondents a beacon of hope that the "American mission" could succeed elsewhere in the world.

Robert Crout explores Lafayette's evolving political discourse on his 1784 and 1824-5 American tours, and his 1829 tour of France. Though they began as celebratory occasions, Lafayette's understanding of the rhetorical potential of his speeches on these tours grew progressively, and he developed a distinct mode of presentation and interaction with the press that presaged the modern "press release." Though the 1784 tour was initially conceived as a celebration of victory, Lafayette ended up consulting with Superintendent of Finances Robert Morris on the Union's economic troubles, advising delegates in Philadelphia as their numbers fell below a quorum and the government risked dissolution, and helping to negotiate a treaty with the Iroquois, all the while developing an increasing sense of the power of his position to push states in the direction of a strong union that culminated in his decidedly political address to the Continental Congress in Trenton and a letter-writing campaign after his return to France. But Lafayette's ambitions were not limited to effecting change in the Americas on that visit: Crout shows that he undertook a careful campaign, aided by a new corps of modern journalists adept at circumventing governmental censorship, to promote liberal reforms in France and to criticize the conservative royalist Bourbon government in France. In France in 1829, as in the American tours, Crout shows that Lafayette used a sophisticated combination of networks of friends and acquaintances and distribution of information and texts from his speeches to local journals and newspapers to maximize the public awareness and impact of his appearances and speeches. Royal attempts to block his appearances backfired as newspapers publicized them and the public invariably sided with Lafayette. Throughout, Lafayette used the new capacity for mass communication arising in both the United States and France to knit together a program of propagation of liberal thought and progressive political change throughout the Atlantic world.

Todd Bourque uses a variety of sources including archival records from Pointe Coupée Parish, Louisiana, to piece together the history of the land grants given to the Marquis de Lafayette in the new United States and his fraught relationship with the nation's Francophone region. For Bourque, the Marquis's Louisiana land grants are a lens through which the governmental and cultural tensions surrounding the incorporation of the Louisiana territory can be seen. Honored with over 12,000 acres for his military service, the land at first allowed the Marquis to settle his debts and reestablish himself after his imprisonment at Olmütz. When the land grant was transferred to the New Orleans area as an inducement to encourage the Marquis to accept the governorship of the new territory, Lafayette's legacy became enmeshed in the politics and cultural history of Louisiana. First his land grant, made under the assumption of rigid geometrical plotting practiced in the rest of the country, was clouded by the overlapping claims and uncertainties of colonial Louisiana surveying practices that followed the landscape and used natural boundaries. Eventually the land grant promise was satisfied primarily with lands in Pointe Coupée Parish, but Lafayette was unsuccessful in profiting from these. It is even unclear whether Lafayette realized he was passing his own lands on a steamship during his 1825 American tour. In spite of his tremendous popularity in the United States and his French and francophone identity, for the newly federated residents of Louisiana, Lafayette, revered for his prominent role in the American Revolution, represented Anglo-American government. Further, the federal appropriation of local lands for the purpose of honoring someone from outside Louisiana struck many residents as an ominous sign, and the claims were embroiled in legal challenges that continued after the Marquis's death.

Michael Martin explores how the image of the Marquis de Lafayette was used differently at different times and places, both by contemporaries and historians. Beginning with the questions of how and why he became such a powerful figure in the mythology of the young republic, Martin traces the historical understanding of Lafayette's character, intellectual path, and accomplishments from the first biographies through the work of Louis

Gottschalk, his twentieth-century biographer, to the modern understanding exemplified by Lloyd Kramer and others in this volume. Tracing the broad arc of Lafayette's image in the United States from the nearly hagiographic accounts that proliferated during his lifetime, Martin examines the shift in the mid-twentieth century to a more cynical view of Lafayette's motives. For Martin, though, Gottschalk introduced a new area of scholarship by acknowledging the mythologizing narratives that surrounded the figure of the Marquis beginning in his own lifetime and opening them up as objects of social and cultural study themselves. Martin then traces the many ways in which modern historians have shown how Lafayette was crucial to the formation of a young republic's self-image and identity. As the greatest hero of the revolution with a true French-American identity, he had a special symbolic role to play in two areas: first, in showing that the American struggle and ideals were part of a larger, Atlantic movement (a point elaborated by Anne Loveland), and, second, in demonstrating the possibility of uniting French and Anglo-American traditions and identity in Louisiana. While the first role has been well explicated by Lloyd Kramer and others, the second is only beginning to be explored, in particular in the essays by Todd Bourque and Sandra Frink in this volume. Martin's own final contribution is to unpack the history of Lafayette's name as a civic marker in Louisiana, from the establishment of Lafayette Parish in 1823 through the Marquis's visit to New Orleans in 1825 and the subsequent naming of a street and a suburb of that city after him to the renaming of Vermilionville as Lafayette in 1884.

Brad Pollock's essay places the Marquis de Lafayette's anti-slavery views in the context of his contemporaries among the founders and other early American commentators. Beginning with his friends George Washington and Thomas Jefferson, Pollock demonstrates how Lafayette was influenced by their ambivalence about the nature of slavery and its place in the American republic, but had the courage to move beyond that ambiguity in ways that his contemporaries did not. For Lafayette, slavery was inherently contradictory to the liberal ideals of freedom and natural rights of men that had inspired the revolution and to which most of his contemporary revolutionary thinkers subscribed. For Pollock, Lafayette's abolitionism falls short of the full-throated moral outrage of such writers as William Lloyd Garrison in the next generation and focuses on the contradiction of ideas and ideals more than on the experience of actual Africans. For Lafayette, as Pollock shows, the outrage of slavery was thoroughly embedded in the structure of the Atlantic world societies: one of Lafayette's most prominent objections to slavery was that it marred the otherwise clear moral mirror held up by the New World to the Old. Though this perspective places Lafayette's abolitionism in the context of his own conception of the balance of moral weight in the Atlantic world and the trajectory of its societies, Pollock also credits Lafayette with arguing a less contextualized critique of racism itself, partly inspired by his friendship with James Armistead. Though he points out the many shortcomings of Lafayette's version of abolitionism, Pollock, like Lloyd Kramer, wishes to move beyond the skepticism of Lafayette's motives so prevalent in most twentieth-century scholarship. In the end, Lafayette emerges from the comparison with Washington and Jefferson as something of a hero of the cause of racial equality, managing to rise above the hypocrisy endemic in the early republic with regard to race and the ideals of freedom and republicanism.

Together, these essays could be said to inaugurate a post-revisionist historiography of Lafayette. By placing Lafayette in a decidedly active, negotiated, multivalent, and multicultural revolutionary Atlantic, these essays go well beyond traditional and revisionist interpretations, situating him in a new context and opening a new stage on which he and other revolutionary figures can now be examined. By showing the many ways that Lafayette was shaped by, actively drew on, and had a profound influence on an astonishing number of social, political, and military events and movements, these essays defy the now hackneyed dichotomy between hagiographic adulation and skeptical dismissal that long dominated interpretations of his life and legacy. It is in many ways fitting that the publication of this volume and the lectures on which it is based should derive from South Louisiana, where paying homage to the many nuances of the relationship between France and the United States, underscoring the often underestimated influence of French thought, language, and traditions in American culture, and exploring the endlessly changing meaning of the French Atlantic are all second nature.

Jordan Kellman
Lafayette, Louisiana

1 Lafayette's Historical Legacy: Politics, Culture, and the Modern World

Lloyd Kramer

The Marquis de Lafayette became one of those rare persons whose life is remembered and discussed on the distant anniversaries of their birth. The most recent, notable anniversary date for Lafayette marked the 250 years since his birth on September 6, 1757, and offered Americans a new opportunity to celebrate his unique role in American history. Special commemorative events took place during 2007 in many of the places that still carry his name—from Lafayette, Louisiana, to Lafayette College in Pennsylvania.[1] More than forty towns and counties in the United States are called Lafayette or Fayette or La-Grange (the name of Lafayette's famous château in France); and "Lafayette" streets can be found throughout America. Although Lafayette also attracted wide popular attention and support at certain moments in French history, he has always been a more popular "hero" in the United States. His important contributions to the American Revolution and his famous friendships with prominent Americans such as George Washington, Thomas Jefferson, and Benjamin Franklin made him a legendary figure before he was thirty years old. Americans viewed Lafayette as their most loyal advocate in Europe, and his national tour of the United States in 1824-25 provoked a remarkable outpouring of early American nationalism.

1. The commemorations in 2007 led to lively discussions of Lafayette's life and ideas in many places around the United States. It was a particular pleasure for me to speak about Lafayette's role in early American history during a visit to the University of Louisiana at Lafayette, where the faculty and students provided a warm welcome and stimulating historical conversations. This essay, however, is a revised version of a paper I presented at Lafayette College as the John L. Hatfield '67 Lecture, which was sponsored by the College's David Bishop Skillman Library on September 6, 2007. I would like to thank Diane Shaw for the invitation to Lafayette's "birthday celebration" in Easton, Pennsylvania. I also want to express my special appreciation to Jordan Kellman for inviting me to participate in the excellent series of Lafayette events at UL-Lafayette and for editing this collection of essays.

The American celebrations of Lafayette's life and legacy in 2007 therefore conveyed the long-existing, popular assumption that Lafayette was an exceptional Frenchman who also embodied distinctive American values and traditions. At the same time, however, the *fêtes* for Lafayette offered new occasions to reflect on his involvement in the wider transitions of modern world history as well as his role in the specific events of the American and French Revolutions. Contemporary historians have tended to ignore or dismiss Lafayette's historical significance, but I want to argue that he continues to merit careful historical attention because he exemplifies decisive changes in modern history and because his participation in these changes left a legacy that is still part of our world. Lafayette is thus an appropriate historical name for twenty-first century towns, counties, schools, and streets, but his significance extends beyond the events of his own lifetime. Many of the political and cultural debates that were important in his era remain important in our world too, and a critical engagement with Lafayette leads into some of the most enduring political and social issues of modern history.

LAFAYETTE AND THE HISTORIANS

Despite his generally positive reputation among most Americans who know about him, Lafayette's stature steadily declined in twentieth-century historical scholarship. As modern historians grew more skeptical about the consequences of political revolutions, the motives of political actors (including America's "founding fathers"), and the personal qualities of Lafayette himself, it was perhaps inevitable that a more ironic, critical view of Lafayette would replace the popular nineteenth-century American descriptions of his life. During most of the first century after his death in 1834, Americans regularly praised Lafayette as their special French friend whose disinterested, high ideals shaped his selfless service in the American Revolution and his later attempts to promote democratic political institutions in Europe. Americans always stressed his close friendship with George Washington and his principled support for American interests on both sides of the Atlantic. In contrast to this highly favorable American reputation, however, Lafayette attracted harsh criticisms in France, where French conservatives saw him as a social traitor to his noble class or the Bourbon monarchy and where French leftists saw him as a national traitor who fled the country when the radical Jacobin revolution began in 1792.[2]

2. I have discussed the evolving American and French historical views of Lafayette in Lloyd S. Kramer, "Lafayette and the Historians: Changing Symbol, Changing Needs,

A more skeptical generation of American historians thus drew on French perspectives as they began to develop a new historical image of Lafayette after the First World War. This new historical portrait depicted Lafayette as a naïve, boyish, vain, and self-interested figure who was never able to reach the highest levels of political or military leadership. Modern academic historians rejected the earlier "great man" theory that had placed him among the giants of world history. John Quincy Adams summarized the prevailing nineteenth-century "great man" view in a famous Congressional eulogy, which portrayed Lafayette as an exceptional "benefactor" to all of mankind and as a unique leader whose contributions to human welfare had never been exceeded "from the creation of the world to this day" in any part of the world.[3] This highly positive, almost god-like image of Lafayette disappeared in the skeptical, modern judgment of twentieth-century writers such as Edward Hyams, who saw in Lafayette "some flaw, some lack of conviction, some indifference to the possible, which makes him, even in his greatest moments, just a little ridiculous." According to Hyams, the famous Hero in Two Worlds "was always tending to make an ass of himself when he put his ideas into action."[4]

This skeptical, ironic view of Lafayette had long circulated in France, but it now echoed through numerous American narratives as well—including, at times, even in Louis Gottschalk's indispensable six-volume biographical study of Lafayette's career down to 1790. Gottschalk took Lafayette seriously as an influential historical figure, but he also tended to stress Lafayette's self-centered attitudes and his deep need for approval from others.[5]

1834-1984," *Historical Reflections/Reflexions historiques* 13 (1984): 373-401. For more on the critical French views, see Patrice Gueniffey, "Lafayette," in *A Critical Dictionary of the French Revolution*, edited by François Furet and Mona Ozouf, translated by Arthur Goldhammer (Cambridge, MA, 1989), 224-33.

3. John Quincy Adams, *Oration on the Life and Character of Gilbert Moitier de Lafayette* (Washington, 1835), 82.

4. Edward Hyams translated a French book by Maurice de La Fuye and Emile Babeau, *The Apostle of Liberty: A Life of Lafayette* (New York and London, 1956). Hyams wrote the introduction to the book, which includes these assessments of Lafayette's career (p. 8); and though the book was published in both the United States and Great Britain, it should be noted that Hyams was English.

5. See, for example, the descriptions of Lafayette's personal traits in Louis Gottschalk, *Lafayette between the American and the French Revolution (1783-1789)* (Chicago, 1950), 428, where Gottschalk describes Lafayette as "essentially self-centered" and as someone whose "need to be approved was so great that he was unable to develop a de-

This view appeared also in the title of another modern biographical study, which described Lafayette simply as a *Statue in Search of a Pedestal.*[6] Although historians have focused on different aspects of Lafayette's career, the critical perspective often comes back to a passing comment by Thomas Jefferson in 1787. Writing to James Madison from Paris about Lafayette's recent public life, Jefferson noted that Lafayette's "foible" was a "canine appetite for popularity."[7] Although Jefferson also made many positive comments about Lafayette (even in this letter to Madison), modern historians have drawn on this one reference to the "appetite for popularity" to diminish the significance of Lafayette's public actions or political commitments.

The modern criticisms of Lafayette's concern for his public reputation typically overlook other aspects of his career, but they make an important point about one of his notable personal characteristics: Lafayette had a constant desire to tell (and hear others tell) his biographical story as a life-long struggle for liberty and human rights. He also liked to be praised, though this is hardly a unique characteristic and in fact is common even among the most successful public figures. His desire for popularity, however, never prevented Lafayette from taking exceptional personal risks to defend his political ideas during every phase of his life in America and France. He paid very high personal and political costs for his beliefs during the French Revolution, the Napoleonic empire, the Bourbon Restoration, and the early July Monarchy. He never simply conformed to the shifting political winds; and if he was a statue in search of pedestals, he was also a statue who never became a weathervane or collapsed when the winds blew hard against him.

The Historical Emergence of the Modern World

It would therefore be easy enough to describe numerous personal and political actions in America and France that would challenge the histori-

---

cent disrespect for the opinions of mankind." And Gottschalk notes that Lafayette "did not fully understand his own motivations or the implications of his own words and actions." Simon Schama expressed a common view when he portrayed Lafayette as "boyish" in his popular history of the French Revolution, *Citizens: A Chronicle of the French Revolution* (New York, 1989), 9-12.

6. Noel B. Gerson, *Statue in Search of a Pedestal: A Biography of the Marquis de La Fayette* (New York, 1976).

7. Thomas Jefferson to James Madison, January 30, 1787, in Julian Boyd, Charles T. Cullen, John Catanzariti, et al., eds. *The Papers of Thomas Jefferson*, 36 vols. to date (Princeton, N. J., 1950-), 11:95.

cal claim that Lafayette regularly made "an ass of himself."[8] My purpose here, however, is not to examine or defend Lafayette's character or personal traits, but to examine instead his legacy as an advocate and symbol of historical changes that we now equate with the development of modern politics and culture. Historians often disagree when they try to identify the starting point for modern history or the components of modernity in different regions of the world. There are nevertheless good historical reasons to argue that many of the decisive transitions to the modern world took place during the years of Lafayette's long life (1757-1834). Despite the inevitable disagreements over key events or periodization, most historians would probably recognize at least eight major, modernizing transitions in Western societies over the decades that we might call, within the analytical framework of this essay, the "Lafayette era." It may be difficult to define the precise chronological boundaries of this transitional historical period, but I would argue that Lafayette's public actions, political beliefs, and personal friendships gave him influential connections with all of his era's most important historical transformations.

First, in the realm of political thought, the crucial change developed through the broad diffusion of Enlightenment-era political theories of human rights (or Natural Rights) and the belief that each individual should have equal legal rights. Although the new theories of human rights were not yet extended to women or non-European peoples, the emerging "logic" of modern political and legal thought challenged old regime, hierarchical systems that had defined rights on the basis of an individual's inherited social

8. I have developed a wide-ranging argument for Lafayette's significant contributions to American and French political life, trans-Atlantic intellectual exchanges, and European liberalism in my book, *Lafayette in Two Worlds: Public Cultures and Personal Identities in an Age of Revolutions* (Chapel Hill, 1996). Other recent accounts of Lafayette's life and career have also provided generally positive assessments of his historical significance. See, for example, James R. Gaines, *For Liberty and Glory: Washington, Lafayette and their Revolutions* (New York, 2007); David A. Clary, *Adopted Son: Washington, Lafayette, and the Friendship that Saved the Revolution* (New York, 2007); Harlow G. Ungar, *Lafayette* (New York, 2002); Jason Lane, *General and Madame de Lafayette: Partners in Liberty's Cause in the American and French Revolutions* (Lanham, MD, 2003); and Paul G. Spalding, *Lafayette: Prisoner of State* (Columbia, SC, 2010). Although these books offer favorable views of Lafayette, it is perhaps notable that the authors are independent scholars or journalists rather than academic historians—except for Spalding, who teaches in a Religion department.

status.[9] Second, the new theories of human rights helped to shape the violent political and military upheavals of the American and French Revolutions, which R. R. Palmer famously described as "The Age of the Democratic Revolution."[10] This general term does not fully convey the contradictions or limits of revolutionary movements that denied political rights to women and protected slavery in America, but it still provides a useful label for the radical political changes that spread across both sides of the Atlantic in the late eighteenth century. Above all, these revolutions established the modern political claim that governments should represent the sovereign will of those whom they govern. Third, the era's violent political revolutions also contributed everywhere to a third crucial development, which can be described most concisely as the rise of nationalism, national identities, and national independence movements. The American revolt against Great Britain was only the first of many national independence movements that emerged in Latin America, Greece, Poland, Italy, and other places where people came to view themselves as oppressed by foreign rulers or empires. Indeed, the pervasive belief in *national* sovereignty and unique *national* cultures would shape the popular themes of all modern nationalisms, which became the world's most powerful political and cultural ideologies in the two centuries after the American and French Revolutions.

A fourth transition was the new political emphasis on individual rights and distinctive national identities that coincided with the cultural emergence of Romanticism. The "Romantics" were highly diverse thinkers and artists, but they all praised the value of individual creativity, the quest for self-realization, and the young "heroes" who fought for their own freedom or the freedom of others. Romanticism tended to celebrate rebellion over conformity to long-existing cultural traditions, and it created a cultural legacy that reshaped modern literature and art—as well as modern images of the artist. This era of political and cultural upheaval also launched a fifth transition, the modern feminist movement—combining arguments for women's political rights with new forms of women's literature, travel writing, and public commentary. Although they could not yet vote or serve in legislative

9. For a perceptive, historical account of how a new eighteenth-century "logic of human rights" transformed political and legal thought during the era of the American and French Revolutions, see Lynn Hunt, *Inventing Human Rights: A History* (New York: W.W. Norton, 2007).

10. R. R. Palmer, *The Age of the Democratic Revolution*, 2 vols. (Princeton, NJ, 1959, 1964). Palmer's book remains the best overall survey of the transatlantic political and ideological upheavals in Lafayette's lifetime.

assemblies, women began to claim a new place in the public sphere by drawing on the political themes of the American and French Revolutions and the cultural themes of early Romanticism. Sixth, the Age of the Democratic Revolution provided a powerful theoretical and political foundation for the development of modern anti-slavery movements, which condemned slavery as a blatant contradiction of human rights and called for the emancipation of all enslaved people. Abolitionist movements also spread across national boundaries and drew on Enlightenment or Romantic theories of individual selfhood and personal freedom.

Seventh, the late eighteenth and early nineteenth centuries became the era of economic "take-off" for a rapidly expanding global trading system. Major changes in this era included the emergence of modern agriculture, the rapid growth of cities, and the establishment of new industries, all of which generated the wealth that would sustain new political democracies and new forms of art and culture. This Industrial Revolution coincided with the age of democratic revolutions and contributed decisively to the creation of the modern world. And finally eighth, the modern transitions that have been noted above all developed through cross-cultural encounters and transnational exchanges. Such exchanges promoted the beliefs in human rights and political revolutions, the emergence of national identities and independence movements, the development of Enlightenment and Romantic cultural movements, the campaigns for women's rights and the abolition of slavery, and the creation of an industrial economy. Complex cross-cultural exchanges thus became increasingly important in the trans-Atlantic interactions of the eighteenth and nineteenth centuries, so that the modern history of "globalization" can be traced back to that era. In contrast to, say, the peasants in medieval European villages, modern people came to define their personal identities and collective aspirations through their expanding contacts with people from other cultures.

This list of significant changes in the emerging modern world could, of course, be extended, and a good historical analysis of these transitions would require much more detail than I have provided here. This brief summary nevertheless suggests why Lafayette's historical era gave him the opportunity to participate in so many important events and cultural changes. Every one of the era's influential historical transitions became part of Lafayette's life, and he also became a public, symbolic advocate for all of them. Historical figures gain wide significance when their lives, actions, and aspirations begin to symbolize collective aspirations or personal beliefs for other people in their own culture and in the cultures of later generations. Lafayette became this kind of symbolic figure during the political and cultural transformations that gradually created the "modern" world. His historical status should therefore be understood as an expression of profound historical changes that he advocated during his lifetime—and which he continued to symbolize after his death. This is not the place to tell again the famous stories of military or political courage that were constantly retold at Lafayette events throughout his American tour in 1824-25. In contrast to the nineteenth-century celebrations of his early military career, however, I want to note briefly how his support for the broader transitions to modernity gave Lafayette both a permanent historical identity and a unique role in the revolutionary upheavals that reshaped the Atlantic world between the 1770s and 1830s.

Lafayette's Role in the Historical Changes of His Era

Lafayette's support for the eighteenth-century theory of natural or inalienable human rights formed a constant theme during every phase of his career. He embraced these theories as a young man and sought to promote his conception of human rights through his highly active involvement in the most important political revolutions of the eighteenth and early nineteenth centuries. As he explained in a letter to the President of the American Philosophical Society when he was inducted into that Society in 1781, Lafayette believed that the American Revolution promoted the "Rights of Mankind" on a "More Liberal Bazis [*sic*]" than any other political movement in the world; and he always envisioned his later public actions as an extension of the political cause he had first supported in America.[11] He therefore introduced the first version of the Declaration of the Rights of Man to France's revolutionary National Assembly on July 11, 1789, emphasizing a commitment to fundamental human rights that he would constantly reiterate in later writings, speeches, and legislative debates.

Lafayette repeatedly argued that the American Revolution had defined "the rights that nature has bestowed on each man, rights that are so inherent to his existence that the entire society has no right to take them from him." He called these inherent human rights "the imprescriptible rights of man and the citizen,"[12] and they included the essential components of human

11. Lafayette to Timothy Matlack, February 15, 1781, in Stanley Idzerda et al., editors, *Lafayette in the Age of the American Revolution: Selected Letters and Papers, 1776-1790*, 5 vols. (Ithaca, NY, 1977-83), 3: 325.

12. This description of human rights appeared in Lafayette's "Reflections" on the French Revolution, which he wrote in 1814; these "Reflections" were later published in

liberty: rights to free speech, to freedom of religion, to free participation in public life, and to freedom from inherited privilege or social hierarchy. He continued to stress the fundamental human right to such freedoms down to the last major speech of his life in 1834, when he reminded the French Chamber of Deputies that "there are natural rights . . . that an entire nation has no right to violate."[13] The doctrine of natural human rights, in short, was the central theme of his entire political philosophy.

This conception of natural rights appeared often in the books of eighteenth-century political theorists, but Lafayette stands out among these theorists as a public figure who carried his ideas directly into military and political action. No one else in that "age of the democratic revolution" played a comparable leading role in both the American and French Revolutions or remained at the center of revolutionary events from 1777 through the French Revolution of 1830. Lafayette participated in the American Revolution mainly through his military actions in the Continental Army, but he also served as a mediator with French government officials, and he always emphasized the close connections between the military and political aspects of the Revolution. His leadership of the decisive Virginia campaign in 1781, for example, became a remarkable early example of revolutionary political warfare. Lafayette avoided direct encounters with the larger army of General Cornwallis during this campaign, and yet he demonstrated that well-equipped British military forces could never break the political will of a small, rag-tag American army (a political conception of warfare that would reappear often in later nationalist movements). The main characteristic of America's revolution, he explained to people in France, had emerged in this new form of popular political struggle. "[N]o European Army would suffer a tenth part of what these troops have," he wrote in one letter about the Americans, but their endurance simply proved "that one must have *citizens* to endure the nakedness, hunger, labors and complete lack of pay that make up the lot of our soldiers. . . ."[14] Lafayette was more connected than any other European with both the common soldiers and the highest leadership of the American revolutionary cause, and he learned from first-hand expe-

---

Marie-Gilbert de Lafayette, *Memoires, correspondance et manuscrits du général Lafayette, publiés par sa famille*, 6 vols. (Paris, 1837-38), 2: 304.

13. Lafayette's speech in the French Chamber of Deputies, January 3, 1834, in ibid., 6: 757.

14. Lafayette to Adrienne de Lafayette, February 2, 1781, in Idzerda et al, *Lafayette in the American Revolution*, 3: 312.

rience how to incorporate political considerations into all of his military campaigns.

This same emphasis on the connections between politics and military affairs shaped his prominent leadership of the Parisian National Guard, which the French National Assembly appointed him to command on the day after the Parisian crowd's assault on the Bastille in July of 1789. He wanted the French to combine their revolutionary campaign for new political rights with a deep respect for law and order and the constitutional actions of the nation's elected representatives. He therefore supported the early French Revolution because he believed that political and military action would achieve the kind of society that he idealistically attributed to the French army in 1792. "Here," he wrote in one of his letters about the revolutionary army, "the principles of liberty and equality are cherished, the laws respected, [and] property is sacred."[15] In Lafayette's view, this combination of liberty, legal equality, and constitutional legislation formed the essential theme of all democratic revolutions. Although he ultimately fled for his life and disappeared into various Prussian and Austrian prisons as the French Revolution entered its most violent phase in 1792, he never doubted that the political principles of the American and early French Revolutions represented universal ideals that modern nations should steadfastly promote in all of their political institutions.[16]

His support for the revolutionary rights of man, however, was linked to his equally fervent support for the rights of national independence. He therefore embraced most of his era's emerging nationalisms, including the independence movements in North and South America and later nationalist movements in Greece, Italy, and Poland. In every case, he supported nationalist opposition to imperial powers: the British and Spanish empires in the Americas or the Ottoman, Russian, and Austrian empires in Europe. If one were to reduce Lafayette's lifelong political actions to a single sentence, one might say simply that he opposed imperial regimes wherever they appeared, and this opposition extended even to Napoleon Bonaparte's imperial regime within France.

Lafayette optimistically assumed that the cause of individual nations would eventually prevail over every imperial system, even when the nationalists' cause seemed to become hopeless in particular historical situations.

15. Lafayette to the Legislative Assembly, June 16, 1792, in Lafayette, *Memoirs*, 3: 329.

16. For a detailed, insightful account of Lafayette's five-year imprisonment between 1792 and 1797, see Spalding, *Lafayette: Prisoner of State*.

This view of ultimate national victories emerged, for example, in a speech at the French Chamber of Deputies during Poland's uprising against the Russian empire in 1831. There were really only two political "categories" in modern Europe, he told his fellow Deputies: "the *oppressors* and the *oppressed*; and I will say . . . ," he went on to explain, "that two principles divide Europe, the *sovereign right of peoples*, and the *divine right of kings*; on one side: *liberty, equality*; on the other: *despotism and privilege*." The campaign for national independence was thus a permanent struggle for the sovereign rights of people, but he was confident that such rights were "in constant progression" and that violent imperial opposition to this cause would only "accelerate its triumph."[17] Lafayette may have downplayed the tension between the rights of individuals and the collective rights of national governments, and yet he clearly understood the rising power of nationalist aspirations in the modern world.

His interest in the distinctive historical aspirations of different nations was typical of the new Romantic nationalism, which merged in many places with a new, nineteenth-century Romantic interest in individual creativity and the "Romantic hero." Lafayette's famous journey to join America's revolutionary struggle for national freedom became a model for later European Romantics, such as Lord Byron, who went off to fight for Romantic conceptions of freedom in Greece and Italy. Although Lafayette always expressed eighteenth-century political ideas, he also became a political hero for nineteenth-century Romantic writers and artists. The imaginative, Romantic writer Mary Shelley summarized this view when she congratulated Lafayette on the French Revolution of 1830 and linked him explicitly to both her own values and the political commitments of her deceased, poetic husband (Percy Shelley). "I was the wife of a man who held dear the opinions you espouse, to which you *were* the martyr and *are* the ornament," she wrote to Lafayette. "I rejoice that the cause to which Shelley's life was devoted, is crowned with triumph."[18]

Similar praise runs through many of the Romantic generation's references to Lafayette, and he reciprocated by praising and supporting the many Romantic writers he knew. He strongly supported Germaine de Staël, James Fenimore Cooper, and the Irish novelist Lady Morgan, but he also provided

17. Lafayette's speech in the French Chamber of Deputies, January 28, 1831, in ibid., 6: 528.

18. Mary Shelley to Lafayette, November 11, 1830, Arthur Dean Collection of Lafayette manuscripts, Division of Rare and Manuscript Collections, Carl A. Kroch Library, Cornell University.

encouragement for Romantic painters such as Ary Scheffer (who painted his portrait in 1822) and the Romantic opera star Maria Malibran.[19] His letters to Malibran, for example, show how the aging, liberal, political leader aligned himself with Romanticism when he reflected on art or music or talented young people. "It is truly painful to love you so much and to be so [far] from you, my dear Maria," he wrote in one of his letters to her after she moved to Belgium in the early 1830s, "[but] remember . . . that my heart is in sympathy with all of your sadness, all your wishes, and that I need your happiness as much as your tenderness."[20] The famous campaigner for political rights and national independence, in other words, readily expressed the sensibilities that circulated in early nineteenth-century Romantic culture.

Lafayette's praise and public support for creative women such as Maria Malibran became another distinctive connection with the emerging movements of modern political and cultural life. After his wife Adrienne died in 1807, Lafayette gradually developed close personal relationships with women who came from diverse national cultures, including Germaine de Staël (French and Swiss), Fanny Wright (Scottish), Cristina Belgiojosa (Italian), Maria Malibran (Spanish), and Lady Morgan (Irish). All of these political and cultural activists became controversial, public symbols of the struggle for women's rights or campaigns for national independence or individual artistic creativity or the movement to abolish slavery. Lafayette's correspondence with his women friends shows that he viewed women as equal participants in the political and cultural movements he supported, and he went well beyond most men of his generation in admiring their independent ideas and actions. The Scottish writer Fanny Wright, who was Lafayette's closest woman friend in the early 1820s and his travel companion during much of his tour through America in 1824-25, reflected on Lafayette's relationships with women when she wrote to him about her political activism. "I dare say you marvel sometimes at my independent way of walking through the world just as if nature had made me of your sex instead of poor Eve's," she noted

19. See, for example, Lafayette to Madame de Staël, 29 Nivôse [Year XII] [January 1804] in Haussonville, ed., "Lettres inédites de La Fayette à Mme de Staël," *Revue des deux mondes*, ser. 7, 6 (November 15, 1921), 316; Lafayette to James Fenimore Cooper, January 8 [1828], in *The Letters and Journals of James Fenimore Cooper*, ed. James Franklin Beard, 6 vols. (Cambridge, MA, 1960-68), 2: 119; and Lafayette to Lady Morgan, November 23, 1818, in the Lafayette Collection, Lilly Library, Indiana University.

20. Lafayette to Maria Malibran, April 10, 1833, in the appendix of documents in Remo Gizaotto, *Maria Malibran (1808-1836): Una vita nei nomi Rossini e Bellini* (Turin, 1986), 563.

in a letter. "Trust me, my beloved friend, the mind has no sex but what habit and education give it, and I . . . have learned . . . to struggle with the elements as any male child of Adam."[21]

Such statements expressed the feisty independence that drew Lafayette to the younger women whom he befriended, and the women definitely believed that he understood and supported their aspirations. His comments to the Italian nationalist Cristina Belgiojosa while she was writing political articles for the French press may be taken as a summary of his warm response to all of the younger women he supported in his later years: "[I admire] your noble character," he wrote in 1831, "[and] your truly sublime qualities, because they are as simple and natural as they are beautiful." He also praised her "generous scorn for wealth, [and her] . . . devotion to liberty," and he emphasized that "I have applauded more than anyone else your determination to depend entirely on yourself. . . ."[22] It is easy to understand why the recipients of such letters appreciated Lafayette's friendship, even if he did not extend his support for women's rights into a political campaign for women's suffrage. His main public action in the campaign to expand women's legal rights emerged in his unsuccessful, nineteenth-century advocacy for the right of French women to divorce their husbands. His liberal women friends, however, recognized that his unbending support for human rights was relevant to all struggles for equality or recognition. Germaine de Staël noted in one of her books that Lafayette was an exceptional French political leader because "power, which has such a great effect in France, has no influence on him; the desire to please in the salons does not alter his conversation in the least; [and] . . . in the prisons of Olmütz as at the pinnacle of influence, he has been equally unshakeable in his attachment to the same principles. . . ."[23] Lafayette thus represented for de Staël an exceptionally principled alternative to Napoleon Bonaparte and other political leaders who pursued their own power at the expense of human rights—which included the right

21. Frances Wright to Lafayette, February 11, 1822, cited in William Randall Waterman, *Frances Wright*, (New York, 1924), 74-75; a copy of the letter (but not the original) is available in the Theresa Wolfson papers at the Labor Documentation Center, Martin P. Catherwood Library, Cornell University.

22. Lafayette to Cristina Belgiojosa, July 13, 1831, in Aldobrandino Malvezzi, *La Principessa Cristina di Belgiojoso*, 3 vols. (Milan, 1936), 1: 305. Malvezzi's biography includes published versions of Belgiojoso's correspondence with Lafayette, which was among the personal papers that her family preserved.

23. Germaine de Staël, *Considerations sur la Revolution française*, edited by Jacques Godechot (Paris, 1983), 180-81.

of women to express themselves as freely as men.

Lafayette's support for human emancipation extended also to the expanding campaign to abolish slavery. His close relationship with Fanny Wright, for example, was built partly on their shared opposition to slavery, which suggests why Lafayette became Wright's strongest supporter when she remained in the United States after 1825 to implement her plan for freeing enslaved people from the southern plantation system. Wright purchased land near Memphis, Tennessee, to establish a planned community (called Nashoba) for enslaved people who would be acquired from slaveholders, trained in artisanal skills, and emancipated to live a free, self-supporting life. Lafayette contributed $8,000 to support Wright's project and wrote his influential American friends to enlist their financial backing. Wright's plan resembled Lafayette's own earlier purchase of a plantation in French Guyana during the 1780s.[24] Much like the project at Nashoba, Lafayette had set out to train and emancipate enslaved people in the French colonies, but his plan collapsed when he lost his land during the French Revolution. Wright's Nashoba experiment also collapsed because she lacked money to sustain the plantation and because her community became notorious for its sexual freedom, its communal economic policies, and its well-publicized hostility to slavery. Lafayette tried to assure friends such as James Madison and the New York banker Charles Wilkes that Wright deserved "high respect for her person, her virtues, intentions and exalted character," though he conceded that she could be "deaf to advice" and "indifferent to the opinions of the world."[25] When Wright eventually traveled to Haiti with almost thirty emancipated slaves, Lafayette continued to praise her abolitionist work, though he was more cautious than Wright during his famous American tour in 1824-25. In the course of this highly publicized tour, however, Lafayette made significant symbolic statements by visiting the African Free School in New York City, meeting in Georgia with an enslaved man whom he had known during the American Revolution, and stressing that African Americans had played an extremely valuable role in the revolutionary campaigns against the

24. Lafayette's plan for the plantation in French Guyana is discussed in Lily Willens, "Lafayette's Emancipation Experiment in French Guyana—1786-1792," in *Transactions of the Sixth International Congress on the Enlightenment* (Oxford, 1983), 222-24; see, also, Gottschalk, *Lafayette between the American and French Revolution*, 218, 244, 262-63.

25. Lafayette to James Madison, October 27, 1827, Dreer Collection, Historical Society of Pennsylvania, and Lafayette to Charles Wilkes, November 28, 1827, Franklin Collection, Beinecke Rare Book and Manuscript Library, Yale University.

British army. He also met a delegation of black men in New Orleans and pointedly remembered that he had "often during the War of Independence seen African blood shed with honor in our ranks for the cause of the United States."[26] Lafayette's opposition to slavery thus remained a central theme in his career, even when it led to disagreements with old American friends such as Thomas Jefferson and James Madison.

Lafayette's critique of slavery became his most notable criticism of the United States, but he had only praise for America's extraordinary economic development. Despite his limited personal interest in commercial activities, Lafayette saw economic expansion as one of the hallmarks of modern, liberal nations. He regularly promoted American-European trade after he returned to France in the 1780s, and he assumed that modern commercial systems required protection of the individual rights and liberties that he supported in his political philosophy. He constantly assured the Americans in 1824-25 that their economic expansion demonstrated the advantages of a modern society in which inherited privileges gave way to equal rights. During his visit to Cincinnati, for example, Lafayette noted that "the wonders of creation and improvement which have happily raised this part of the Union to its high degree of importance, prosperity and happiness have been to me . . . a continued object of attention and delight."[27] Economic growth, as Lafayette often confirmed in his American speeches, was transforming the North American continent and providing a model for modern, commercial development in other parts of the world. "Nothing indeed can be more gratifying," he explained in another speech, " . . . than to consider what this beautiful, fertile part of America . . . was doomed for ages to remain under the anti-social governments of the European courts . . . and to compare it

26. The visits to the African Free School in New York and the slave in Georgia were described in newspaper reports in the New York *Commercial Advertiser*, September 11, 1824 (which were republished in *Lafayette, Guest of the Naion: A Contemporary Account of the Triumphal Tour of General Lafayette through the United States in 1824-25, as Reported by the Local Newspapers*, ed. Edgar Ewing Brandon, 3 vols. [Oxford, Ohio, 1950-57] 1: 196-97) and in the *Savannah Georgian*, March 24, 1825 (which were republished in A *Pilgrimage of Liberty: A Contemporary Account of the Triumphal Tour of General Lafayette through the Southern and Western States in 1825, as Reported by the Local Newspapers*, ed. Edgar Ewing Brandon (Athens, OH, 1944), 106. His statement to black veterans in New Orleans appears in the *Courier de la Louisiane*, April 19, 1825 (also published in Brandon, *Pilgrimage of Liberty*, 182).

27. Lafayette's reply to welcome in Cincinnati, *Liberty Hall and Cincinnati Gazette*, May 21, 1825, in Brandon, *Pilgrimage of Liberty*, 323.

with the creations, improvements, [and] splendid prospects which have been the rapid result of republican principles. . . ."[28] In contrast to many European radicals, Lafayette did not endorse early socialist theories or criticize the social consequences of capitalism and industrialization. On the contrary, he favored transnational commerce as a key component of modern social and political advancement—much as he saw the transnational movement of liberal political principles and Romantic cultural themes as essential contributions to human progress.

All of Lafayette's support for political revolutions, for Romantic artists, for women and the human rights of enslaved people, and for commercial development were ultimately linked to his transnational conception of modern human societies. Lafayette was constantly introducing Americans to French friends or sending French publications to friends in the United States, bringing travelers from Greece, Spain, Poland, and America to his dinner table at LaGrange, and stressing the interconnection of people in all parts of the world. His letters were filled with comments about people in different nations, but here two examples will serve to show how Lafayette participated in what we now call cross-cultural exchanges and the development of transnational identities.

The first example comes from an anonymous memoir that a young visitor wrote after attending Lafayette's Parisian salon in the early 1830s. The author described Lafayette as an international "flag of civilization" who drew to himself the "patriots from every country"—patriots "who, after fighting in vain for the liberty of their own countries had come to France in search of refuge and hopes for the future" and who turned to Lafayette as the representative "of the new era that had begun with the July Revolution." As the anonymous visitor described it, an evening at Lafayette's apartment offered opportunities to meet the people from America, Poland, Italy, Spain, Belgium, Portugal, Ireland, and England who had come to "render homage to the leader of civilization and to receive from him the investiture of liberty."[29] We may smile ironically at this somewhat naive image of the multinational idealists at Lafayette's apartment, but this youthful author emphasized Lafayette's unique importance in the international campaigns

28. Lafayette's reply to welcome in Natchez, *Mississippi Gazette*, April 23, 1825, in Brandon, *Pilgrimage of Liberty*, 207.

29. Memoir entitled "Le général Lafayette, soirées à son hôtel," at the Archives Nationales [Paris], carton 252 AP 2, pièce 221. The anonymous author notes that he (it seems to have been written by a young man) wrote the memoir on October 25, 1831, in Norwich, England, but the author never reveals his identity.

for early nineteenth-century liberalism and nationalism. Lafayette always defined his public role as a prolonged campaign to support these transnational political movements, as we can see in his vehement public support for Poland's national revolution against the Russian empire in 1831-32. The Poles responded by making him an honorary officer of the Polish National Guard, and Lafayette offered shelter for Polish exiles who escaped to France after the revolutionary movement was suppressed. He also emphasized his personal identification with international political movements at Parisian meetings of the displaced Poles.

> It is in the name of . . . all the Polish Committees of France, and in the name of the American committee, representing the Polish associations of the other hemisphere [he announced at one of these meetings] . . . [that I] welcome the first of our brother exiles who have arrived in the capital. May the hospitable and sympathetic land of France become for them a second country, without allowing this adoption . . . to cause them any loss of the inalterable nationality which was in all times their glory and their salvation.[30]

This typical Lafayette greeting thus began with his long-held belief that people in different nations shared similar political aspirations, even though he assumed that each society also had an "inalterable nationality" that gave individual exiles both "their glory and salvation." The Polish exiles exemplified the kinds of international migrations, national identities, and transnational political allegiances that became common in modern history and in the cross-cultural exchanges that characterized every phase of Lafayette's career. Here, too, as in so many other aspects of his long life, we can see the enduring connections between Lafayette's story and the wider changes or conflicts in modern societies.

Lafayette's Symbolic Significance in the Twenty-first Century

It would be possible to add other examples, but it should be apparent by now that we can readily identify numerous historical continuities between Lafayette's life and many of the key political or cultural values in our own society: the commitments to equal human rights, the belief in the national

30. Lafayette's address of November 29, 1831, in Comte D'Angeberg [pseudonym of Leonard Chodzko], *Recueil des traités, conventions et actes diplomatiques concernant la Pologne, 1762-1862* (Paris, 1862), 893-94.

sovereignty of peoples rather than the sovereignty of kings, the struggles of women and diverse racial groups to achieve social equality, the support for individual creativity, the belief in economic development, and the openness to cross-cultural exchanges. Yet there is one other central theme in Lafayette's life that seems to be rapidly disappearing in early twenty-first century Western societies: his unshakeable optimism about the future of democratic politics.[31] Lafayette and his liberal friends believed that the political reforms and revolutions of their generation would lead to a better and freer world. From the perspective of our own disillusioned, skeptical era, the most distinctive political theme of the "age of the democratic revolution" may well be found in the optimistic belief that the aspiration for more democratic institutions can be put into practice through new political movements and sustained political action. Our own post-revolutionary age has grown far more pessimistic about modern political life, which is commonly viewed as either corrupt or indifferent to the ideals of an open, participatory democratic system. In short, the political expectations of Lafayette and his revolutionary generation can often seem naïve in the context of our own special-interest, big-money political culture.

Yet, at the risk of embracing Lafayette's alleged naiveté myself, I want to propose that his aspirations are still worth considering as we look for a path through our own, more cynical, political culture. Lafayette and his political allies remind us that politics should be a sphere for implementing ideals such as freedom, justice, democracy, and broad social interests rather than simply a media circus of manipulated fears, big-money favors, and personal gossip. Although the "public sphere" seems increasingly irrelevant to individual aspirations in our skeptical, fragmented, celebrity-obsessed culture, political decisions still affect private lives, and political movements can still mobilize broad public support when they express social concerns that transcend narrow forms of self-interest. Lafayette's optimism about the value of political ideas and actions therefore offers a forceful, critical alternative to the rampant cynicism in contemporary democratic nations such as France and the United States.

It would of course be dangerous to live in our world without the skeptical, critical perspectives on human self-delusion and self-interest that come from an ironic view of historical leaders and political institutions. Irony and

31. The themes and much of the language in this paragraph and the following two paragraphs draw directly from the epilogue of my previously cited book, *Lafayette in Two Worlds*, 276-79. I return to these themes here because they summarize my view of Lafayette's legacy in the contemporary world.

cynicism help expose the delusions, hypocrisies, and deceptions that appear in all political cultures. Perhaps, though, we can also continue to draw upon the history and ideas of Lafayette's optimistic generation as we confront the apparently intractable problems of our own post-revolutionary society and government. In contrast to much of our contemporary skepticism, Lafayette and his friends believed that political institutions could change, that the future could be better than the past, that political and legal equality would be better than traditional social hierarchies, that tolerance would be better than repression, that the human rights of individuals should not be sacrificed to the sovereign rights of nations, and that private happiness could not finally survive without strong commitments to the public good. Debates about these ideas have shaped much of modern history, and we can expect the debates to continue in the future political cultures of most nations. If we choose to dismiss Lafayette's ideas as naïve or absurdly romantic, however, we will also be choosing to abandon our most valuable democratic legacy from the past as well as our own aspirations for a better, more democratic future. And if we forget about Lafayette's ideas and political struggles, there will be little reason to celebrate future anniversaries of Lafayette's birth.

I believe, however, that people will continue to mark the chronological milestones that evoke the memory of Lafayette's long struggle for human rights and provoke new debates about his historical legacy. Equally important, the memories of Lafayette's actions, setbacks, and aspirations should give historical encouragement to people who will be fighting the political battles to come. Lafayette's legacy will not disappear because future generations will surely have to make their own contributions to the endless, modern campaigns to protect and expand the human rights of all persons, no matter where they may live or what injustices they may confront.

2 History, Heroes, and National Identity: The Marquis de Lafayette's Visit to New Orleans in 1825

Sandra Frink

In 1825, a citizen of New Orleans asserted that the celebrations "which took place in the United States on account of General La Fayette, bore a character of universal affection" and "were the object of the general consent of all classes of society, which in each State was made a family festival, and for all, a National one."[1] When Lafayette stepped onto the shores of the United States in 1824 as the "guest of the nation," he cemented his place as a hero of the American Revolution who embodied the virtues that helped forge the nation and its citizens. In the words of historian Lloyd Kramer, the "Lafayette Narrative," created during his thirteen-month tour of the states in 1824 and 1825, "tended to fuse the meaning of Lafayette with the meaning of America."[2] Certainly, in many cities along the Atlantic Seaboard, where links to the Revolution's history were both familial and spatial, this connection resonated among the inhabitants. The circumstances that shaped his visit to New Orleans in April 1825, however, proved to be much more complicated. His visit to the city prompted a public and often acrimonious debate over the meaning of American identity and of the city's own position in the nation. Ethnic and racial rivalries exploded as competing groups attempted to claim a link to the hero and his history. The most elaborate civic celebration of the pre-Civil War Era in New Orleans also proved to be its most divisive, providing insight into how its citizens conjoined national loyalty with local sentiment and personal heritage.

As the people of New Orleans anxiously awaited the arrival of Lafayette, they reflected on their own relationship with the hero and the ideals he rep-

1. A Citizen of New Orleans, *Visit of General Lafayette to Louisiana, Containing the Speeches Addressed to Him, with his Answers* (New Orleans: M. Cruzat, State Printer, 1825), 32.

2. Lloyd Kramer, *Lafayette in Two Worlds: Public Cultures and Personal Identities in an Age of Revolution* (Chapel Hill: University of North Carolina Press, 1996), 193.

resented. Since its entry into the Union in 1812, New Orleans had witnessed a dramatic increase in population, as Anglo-American migrants from the east joined a population of Creoles who drew their cultural and political inspiration from an admixture of French, Spanish, African, and Caribbean influences.[3] Controversies between various factions in the city during the intervening years often centered on whether its citizens, particularly the Latin Creoles, professed sincere loyalty to the principles of the nation. Not surprisingly, therefore, the visit of Lafayette in 1825 provoked heated controversy over

3. Perhaps one of the most debated issues among scholars of New Orleans has been the definition of "Creole." Although it is often generically used to denote native-born residents of the Americas, regardless of color or national heritage, certain groups have claimed the identity to the exclusion of others. Specifically, in the years leading up to the Civil War, and most prominently during Reconstruction, white writers of Creole ancestry began to argue that in Louisiana the term referred exclusively to native-born whites of European ancestry. This creation of what Joseph Tregle refers to as the "Creole myth" has informed much of the work on Louisiana during the early twentieth century, and continues even today in many historical studies. Tregle and others have demonstrated that most inhabitants of the city in the early nineteenth century used the term "Creole" to denote all natives of the state, regardless of color or ancestry. Joseph G. Tregle, Jr., "Creoles and Americans," in *Creole New Orleans: Race and Americanization*, ed. Arnold R. Hirsch and Joseph Logsdon (Baton Rouge: Louisiana State University Press, 1992), 131-45; Joseph G. Tregle, Jr., "Early New Orleans Society: A Reappraisal," *Journal of Southern History* 18 (February 1952), 21-36. Studies that generally concur with this interpretation include Gwendolyn Midlo Hall, *Africans in Colonial Louisiana: The Development of Afro-Creole Culture in the Eighteenth Century* (Baton Rouge: Louisiana State University Press, 1992), 157-59; Arnold R. Hirsch and Joseph Logsdon, "Preface," in *Creole New Orleans: Race and Americanization*, ed. Arnold R. Hirsch and Joseph Logsdon (Baton Rouge: Louisiana State University Press, 1992), xi; and Sybil Klein, "Introduction," in *Creole: The History and Legacy of Louisiana's Free People of Color*, ed. Sybil Klein (Baton Rouge: Louisiana State University Press, 2000), xiii-xvii. Unlike Tregle, Virginia Dominquez argues that the Foreign French may be incorporated into the category of white Creoles because of their close affiliation in *White by Definition: Social Classification in Creole Louisiana* (New Brunswick: Rutgers University Press, 1986); John M. Sacher adopts a more restrictive use of the term Creole, limiting it to those born in Louisiana of exclusively French or Spanish descent, in his book *A Perfect War of Politics: Parties, Politicians, and Democracy in Louisiana, 1824-1861* (Baton Rouge: Louisiana State University Press, 2003), 11. In this paper, I use "Latin Creole" to refer to native-born New Orleans residents of French or Spanish heritage who considered themselves white. When discussing native born men and women of mixed Spanish, French, or African heritage, I use the term Creoles of color.

who in the city could rightfully claim an association with the revered General and the history he embodied. It also inspired numerous groups typically marginalized in civic ceremonies, including free men of color and Native Americans, to demand recognition for their contributions to the nation. It proved, in fact, to be the most inclusive public ceremony held in New Orleans prior to the Civil War.[4]

Lafayette's visit to New Orleans offers a striking opportunity to explore the racial, ethnic, and religious divisions between Latin Creoles, Anglo-Americans, free people of color, and Native Americans that informed the political and social landscape of the city in the first decades of the nineteenth century. Furthermore, it demonstrates that while in theory such celebrations sought to unite disparate segments of the population around a common national sentiment, in practice local issues and disputes often informed and shaped conceptions of their national identity. Members of each group in New Orleans that sought an audience with the Marquis drew from their pasts to craft a narrative of valor and virtue that demonstrated their own particular allegiance to the revolutionary ideals Lafayette had helped secure. For Anglo-Americans who had migrated to New Orleans since its acquisition in the Louisiana Purchase, Lafayette's visit became a means of forging a link between their newly adopted city and the communities they had left behind. Latin Creoles, meanwhile, underscored their shared cultural heritage with the general and self-consciously trumpeted their valor during the War of 1812. For male members of the free militia of color and the Choctaw nation, the visit became a means to reaffirm their contributions to the prosperity and security of the nation and to protest their increasing exclusion from the polity. Despite the unequal degree of power men in New Orleans could claim within the political system, all were allowed a forum to voice their concerns and script their own narrative of patriotism and honor. Women, meanwhile, found themselves cast to the sidelines. Once granted a prominent role as proud, Republican mothers during civic celebrations, they now sat silently along the edges of the ceremonies, resigned to waving their handkerchiefs from balconies. Analyzing this celebration from the perspective of each group enables us to understand how the social and political landscape of the 1820s became intertwined with each group's relationship to the history of Lafayette and to the history of the country.

4. Although slaves undoubtedly participated in the celebration, their activities and voices remain absent in the records. This paper will focus exclusively on free men and women in New Orleans during the ceremony.

* * *

Almost as soon as Lafayette accepted the invitation by President Monroe and Congress to visit the United States, preparations for his arrival became a national preoccupation and a "formidable undertaking," as people throughout the union organized celebrations in their cities and towns. The United States Congress, as a means of thanking Lafayette for his service to the country during the Revolution, voted to pay him $200,000 upon his arrival and offered him a land grant in any part of the United States.[5] Lafayette recognized his role, both as an icon of the Revolution and a unifying symbol of the nation he had adopted as his own, spiritually if not physically.[6] As the first "Guest of the Nation," Lafayette visited every state in the Union over thirteen months, and became the first public figure to take "such a long and comprehensive tour of the United States."[7]

The significance of Lafayette's visit to the nation was felt profoundly by the citizens of New Orleans, who sought to be among the first to extend him an invitation.[8] The state spared no cost to provide a reception worthy of his honor, eventually granting $15,000 towards the celebration in New Orleans.[9] As a city that was consistently derided by both tourists and residents as "foreign," the visit of the Marquis de Lafayette provided its residents a means to demonstrate their patriotic fervor.[10] Some historians have even marked

5. Edgar Ewing Brandon, ed., *A Pilgrimage of Liberty: A Contemporary Account of the Triumphal Tour of General Lafayette* (Athens, OH: The Lawhead Press, 1944), 13-15, quotation 14; Francis Burns, "Lafayette Visits New Orleans," *Louisiana Historical Quarterly* 29, no. 2 (April 1946): 297; Kramer, 186-87.

6. Anne C. Loveland, *Emblem of Liberty: The Image of Lafayette in the American Mind* (Baton Rouge: Louisiana State University Press, 1971), 74-76; Patricia Brady, "Carnival of Liberty: Lafayette in Louisiana," *Louisiana History* 41, no. 1 (Winter 2000), 26-27.

7. Brandon, ed., 14.

8. Ibid., 160.

9. Albert E. Fossier, *New Orleans: The Glamour Period, 1800-1840* (1957; reprint, Gretna, LA: Pelican Publishing Company, 1998), 496.

10. Numerous travelers noted that New Orleans most resembled a foreign, and particularly a European, city throughout the decades before the Civil War. See, for example, Sir Charles Lyell, *A Second Visit to the United States of North America*, vol. 2 (New York: Harper & Brothers, 1849), 111; Henri Herz, *My Travels in America*, trans. Henry Bertram Hill (Madison: State Historical Society of Wisconsin, 1963), 83; Frederick Law Olmstead, *The Cotton Kingdom: A Traveller's Observations on Cotton and Slavery in the American Slave States*, vol. 1 (New York: Mason Brothers, 1861), 291; Timothy Flint,

the visit as the pivotal moment when the people of New Orleans became "American."[11] Certainly, the celebration for Lafayette, like other civic celebrations staged by the city during the nineteenth century, sought to pacify, at least temporarily, factions and rivalries around a common national sentiment and purpose. The visit, however, did not erase or even ease existing political rivalries, but rather served as a means of reaffirming the divisions that structured local politics.

Politics in New Orleans during the early 1820s centered primarily on the conflicts between Creoles, who sought to maintain the power they held in the city prior to its transfer to the United States, and Anglo-Americans, who strove to recast New Orleans into a city that more closely resembled the Eastern Seaboard cities of their birth. As John M. Sacher has noted, the Creoles crafted the 1812 state constitution in a way that would ensure their continued influence despite the growing percentage of Anglo-Americans in the population. Considered conservative and even aristocratic by its critics, the constitution limited suffrage and office holding to a group of elite leaders within the community who could command the greatest loyalty among constituents. As a result, ethnic ties, rather than political party affiliation, de-

---

Recollections of the Last Ten Years (Boston: Cummings, Hilliard and Company, 1826), 291; De Witt C. Roberts. *Southern Sketches, or Eleven Years Down South, Including Three Years in Dixie* (Jacksonville, FL: D.W. Roberts, Publisher, 1865), 17-18; James Logan, *Notes of a Journey through Canada, the United States of America, and the West Indies* (Edinburgh: Fraser and Company, 1838), 177-78; Timothy Flint, *History and Geography of the Mississippi Valley*, vol. 1 (Cincinnati: E.H. Flint, 1833), 265.

11. Brady, 40; Due to its diverse composition, historians have often characterized New Orleans as different from other cities in the United States, even "foreign" and "unique." Historians disagree over when the city became "American," dating it to 1803 and the transfer of the territory to the United States, to 1815 and the Battle of New Orleans, to 1825 with the visit of the Marquis de Lafayette, to 1852, when the city unified and the Anglo-Americans in the city wrested political power from the Latin Creoles, and even to the 1857 celebration of Mardi Gras. See, for example, Joseph Ingersoll, *Mammon and Manon in Early New Orleans: The First Slave Society in the Deep South, 1718-1819* (Knoxville: University of Tennessee Press, 1999), xix; Robert V. Remini, *The Battle of New Orleans: Andrew Jackson and American's First Military Victory* (New York: Viking, 1999), 187-90; Tregle, "Creoles and Americans," 173; James Gill, *Lords of Misrule: Mardi Gras and the Politics of Race in New Orleans* (Jackson: University Press of Mississippi, 1997); Some scholars, including Joseph Roach, have suggested that Latin New Orleans experienced both Anglification and Africanization, a process which "continues to be reenacted in the streets." Joseph R. Roach, *Cities of the Dead: Circum-Atlantic Performance* (New York: Columbia University Press, 1996), 10.

termined how Creoles and, some argued, Anglo-Americans, cast their votes and ensured that local and state, rather than national, elections garnered the most interest.[12]

The celebrations surrounding Lafayette's visit became a public manifestation of their significance to the populace. Historians have demonstrated that although civic celebrations bring disparate citizens together to share in a common nationalist spirit, they also serve as a forum to debate their respective claims to its meaning and legacy. Such divisions, far from disqualifying members of the polity as proper nationals, shape both the events and their social and political meaning. Conflict, and specifically the politicization of national rituals, therefore, more accurately characterizes the practice of nationalism.[13] The contentious civic ceremonies staged by the people of New Orleans demonstrated their commonality with others in the nation, even as their particular expressions of "American identity" underscored the unique composition of the city's residents. While each group sought an audience with Lafayette in their own interests, rather than as a collective body, their participation in this civic event crafted a national identity distinctly defined by local circumstance.

The visit of Lafayette allowed the Latin Creoles of New Orleans to both celebrate their common heritage with the General and prove to their detractors that they were fit for republican citizenship. An anonymous "citizen of New Orleans," whose sympathies clearly lay with the Creole community, wrote an account of Lafayette's visit that drew a sharp distinction between the civic ceremonies of Europe and those in the United States. Perhaps hoping to affirm the Latin Creole's recognition of this contrast, he noted that "in Europe . . . the citizens are merely spectators of the ceremonies, the object of which is, rather to show the pageantry of the sovereign, than to testify the joy of the people." He continued by proudly declaring that "with us, it is quite

12. Sacher, 10-12.

13. For studies of civic ceremonies as expressions of nationalism see, David Waldstreicher, *In the Midst of Perpetual Fetes: The Making of American Nationalism, 1776-1820* (Chapel Hill: University of North Carolina Press, 1997); Simon P. Newman's argument is similar to that of Waldstreicher, but his study focuses exclusively on parades. Simon P. Newman, *Parades and the Politics of the Street: Festive Culture in the Early American Republic* (Philadelphia: University of Pennsylvania Press, 1997); Susan G. Davis, *Parades and Power: Street Theatre in Nineteenth Century Philadelphia* (Philadelphia: Temple University Press, 1986); Mary Ryan focuses on New York, San Francisco and New Orleans in *Civic Wars: Democracy and Public Life in the American City during the Nineteenth Century* (Berkeley: University of California Press, 1997).

the contrary." In the United States, he asserted, public festivals were "only the expression of the people's sentiments, and only the effect of their will," since "every one puts himself forward to co-operate in giving them all the splendor possible."[14] By acknowledging these differences, he made it clear to readers that the Latin Creoles of New Orleans fully embraced the democratic spirit of the event.

Latin Creoles in New Orleans nevertheless feared that their efforts to demonstrate their devotion to liberty would be deemed inadequate. Many city leaders despaired over the fact that New Orleans, unlike cities in the Northeast, still resembled a frontier town. Mayor Louis Philippe de Roffignac, born to an aristocratic French family that had fled the guillotine in the midst of the French Revolution, was one such leader who believed it incumbent upon the citizens to demonstrate their adherence to the patriotic ideals Lafayette embodied. He worried that New Orleans would not be able to show Lafayette "anything which could come near, even from afar, the splendor and magnificence displayed everywhere on his passage." He continued: "We have no Capitol, no fortifications, no navy, no arsenals for him to admire; no public establishment, no building deserving his attention."[15] In addition to fearing that their city was backward, many Creoles felt painfully self-conscious about their absence during the American Revolution. While they shared a unique heritage with Lafayette, they could not claim to have fought for liberty and republicanism at the nation's founding.

Unable to share in Lafayette's glory during the Revolution and despondent over their city's lack of civic splendor, the Latin Creoles of New Orleans chose instead to highlight their role in defeating the British during the country's second "revolution," the War of 1812. As Mayor Roffignac indicated, "we have here . . . only our deepest sentiments *and the battlefields* where a handful of these brave Americans that he loves have gloriously protected their homes."[16] For many Creoles in New Orleans, the 1815 victory in the Battle of New Orleans solidified their standing as American nationals and proved to those who questioned their allegiance that they would support the United States. Their desire to highlight this contribution to American free-

14. While the author of this document remains anonymous, it is clear from the tone and sentiment expressed throughout that he was a member of the Creole community. A Citizen of New Orleans, 32.

15. New Orleans City Council, *Messages from the Mayor* (translations), January 26, 1825, New Orleans Public Library (hereafter NOPL).

16. Ibid.

dom prompted their decision to welcome Lafayette not in the city, but rather at the Chalmette Battle Grounds, where the Louisiana Militia had joined with another American hero, Andrew Jackson, to battle against the British.

The link forged between the War of 1812, however, and the patriotism of the Creoles contained its own conflicts. For this reason, it is worth stepping back to consider what occurred during and after the battle, for it both shaped and informed the celebration for Lafayette. In 1812, the residents of New Orleans had only recently and rather reluctantly accepted their federally appointed governor, William C.C. Claiborne, and remained suspicious of the Anglo-Americans who began moving into their city. These suspicions were not unwarranted. Many recently arrived Anglo-Americans believed that the Creoles of New Orleans and the rest of Louisiana were "the most radically and essentially unfit" for self-government.[17] The burden of alleviating the suspicions of Creoles rested on Claiborne, a Protestant from Virginia. He also faced the problem of imposing American laws and culture on a predominantly French-speaking, Catholic citizenry accustomed to European common law.[18] He recognized the precarious balance he needed to maintain between respecting the wishes of the native inhabitants and overseeing the transition to republican government. By carefully courting leaders in the Creole community, he slowly gained their confidence.

Claiborne's faith in Creole loyalty, however, became more tentative during the War of 1812, particularly when the battles moved closer to the city. In his letters, he continually voiced concern that the Creoles would support the British rather than the United States, a concern that was fueled by the propaganda circulated in the city by the British army.[19] General Andrew Jackson exacerbated the situation by questioning both the loyalty of the militia

17. Quoted in Sacher, 13.

18. See, for example, William C.C. Claiborne to James Madison, January 2, 1804, in Dunbar Rowland, ed. *Official Letter Books of William C.C. Claiborne, 1801-1816*, vol. 6 (Jackson, MS: State Department of Archives and History, 1917), 330; Ferdinand Stone, "The Law with a Difference and How it Came About," in *The Past as Prelude: New Orleans, 1718-1968*, ed. Hodding Carter (New Orleans: Tulane University, 1968), 42-70.

19. For letters in which William C.C. Claiborne expresses his concerns, see, for example, Claiborne to Andrew Jackson, October 24, 1814, in Rowland, ed., 288-89; Claiborne to Honorable Eligius Fromentin, October 24, 1814, in Rowland, ed., 285-86; See also Charles Gayarré, *History of Louisiana*, vol. 4 (1882; reprint, Gretna: Pelican Publishing, 1974), 341; Colonel Nicholls to the Inhabitants of Louisiana, August 29, 1814 and August 31, 1814, Edward Nicholls and William H. Percy Letters, Historic New Orleans Collection (hereafter HNOC).

and of the Creole residents. His vigilant enforcement of martial law in the city led to the arrest of many innocent and respected civilians, who then often languished in the city's prison for weeks. Meanwhile, American troops stationed near New Orleans persistently demonstrated their lack of respect for the Louisiana militia, which caused outrage among the populace. According to Jonathon Rees, a Major in the 15th Regiment of the Louisiana militia, Jackson similarly showed little respect for the local troops. When Jackson visited his company, composed of many respected Latin Creoles, he reportedly "paid very little attention to either officers or men," prompting Rees to write, "We may conclude from that what he thinks of us."[20]

Concerns over the patriotism of the populace were set aside for a brief but significant moment when the diverse population of Creoles, Anglo-Americans, free people of color, immigrants, and slaves joined with soldiers from Tennessee and Kentucky to celebrate their victory over the British in the Battle of New Orleans on January 8, 1815.[21] Nevertheless, the Creoles of the city made sure that the ceremony highlighted their contribution to the victory and their power in the city. The civic ceremony took place in the Place d'Armes, the political, social, and spiritual center of the Creole city. Surrounding the square was the government building, the Cabildo, and the center of the city's religious life, the St. Louis Cathedral. Ironically, this square, which would become synonymous with the Creoles of New Orleans during the nineteenth century, would later be renamed Jackson Square after the decidedly American hero who had stridently questioned their patriotism.[22] In the coming decades, the square was alternately celebrated as

20. Jonathon Rees to David Rees, December 11, 1814, David Rees Papers, Tulane University Special Collections (hereafter TUSC); Matthew Warshauer, "The Battle of New Orleans Reconsidered: Andrew Jackson and Martial Law," *Louisiana History* 39, no. 3 (Summer 1998): 262-75; City Council records also indicate that fights between members of the Louisiana militia and the US Navy stationed in New Orleans occurred during the war. New Orleans City Council, *Official Proceedings* (translations), vol. 2, bk. 4, January 21, 1813, NOPL.

21. Remini, 72; Arsène Lacarrière Latour, *Historical Memoir of the War in West Florida and Louisiana in 1814-1815* (1816, reprint, Gainesville: University of Florida Press, 1964), 89-92.

22. Over time, the Place d'Armes and the streets surrounding it became increasingly associated with the Creole population, those people who could trace their ancestry to the colonial period. In an attempt to revive this area of the city in the 1840s, the Countess de Pontalba, the daughter of Don Andres Almonester y Roxas and a powerful Creole citizen, built row houses on either side of the square to attract business to the area. She

the spiritual center of the city and derided as being "anti-American." The celebration itself appeared to some to be characteristically "Creole." One observer, for example, suggested that it "displayed the talent of the French in devising emblematic shows."[23] The people of New Orleans certainly went to greater lengths than those in other cities to commemorate the end of the war, a tradition that would continue throughout the antebellum era.

Despite the momentary euphoria created by the victory, however, distrust and fragmentation quickly severed the precarious alliance formed between the inhabitants of the city. By March 2, 1815, less than three months after the Battle and celebration, Governor Claiborne conceded that "the union and mutual confidence which so recently pervaded the whole community no longer exists."[24] During the following decade, various factions battled for recognition and honor in the city's public life and during local, state, and national elections. When Andrew Jackson ran for president in 1824, many Creoles chose to support Clay or Adams, refusing to forget the slights they had received a decade earlier. Anglo-Americans, by contrast, overwhelmingly supported Jackson because of his role in saving the city. The campaigns were dominated by charges that the Creoles of New Orleans were unfit for republican government and tainted by their monarchical heritage. The obvious hyperbole of such claims notwithstanding, the Creoles did little to alleviate Anglo concerns when they elected Dominique Bouligny to the Senate in 1824. Bouligny, a Creole from New Orleans, did not speak English.[25]

It was in this context that the people of New Orleans prepared for the arrival of the Marquis de Lafayette and the civic celebration to be held in his honor. As planned, the people of the city gathered at the Chalmette Battleground to welcome Lafayette when he arrived on April 9, 1815. They then

---

was instrumental in changing the name of the square to Jackson Square in 1851 and contributed a significant portion of the money used to erect the statue in his honor. Christina Vella, *Intimate Enemies: The Two Worlds of the Baroness de Pontalba* (Baton Rouge: Louisiana State University Press, 1997), 273-74; Stanley Clisby Arthur, *Old New Orleans: Walking Tours of the French Quarter* (1936; reprint, Gretna, LA: Pelican Publishing Company, Inc., 1995), 110-111, 122-25; Right Reverend Celestine M. Chambon, "The St. Louis Cathedral and its Neighbors," 2nd ed. rev. and ed. by James J.A. Fortier (New Orleans: Louisiana State Museum, October 10, 1938), 109-112, New Orleans Collection Pamphlets, Tulane University Special Collections.

23. Major A. Lacarrière Latour quoted in Remini, 187.

24. William C.C. Claiborne to James Monroe, March 2, 1815, in Rowland, ed., 349.

25. Sacher, 25; Joseph G. Tregle, Jr., *Louisiana in the Age of Jackson: A Clash of Cultures and Personalities* (Baton Rouge: Louisiana State University Press, 1999), 116.

proceeded to the Montgomery plantation, which had served as General Jackson's headquarters during the War of 1812.[26] Upon receiving Lafayette, the Anglo-American governor, Henry S. Johnson, appeared "evidently much agitated." The newspaper reported that "the scene was imposing; the field of the battle of the eighth of January was in sight; and before him stood the warrior of Brandywine and of York."[27] The governor conceded that Louisiana "did not share with you in the toils and glory of the war of independence." Nevertheless, he made a point of stressing that "her inhabitants are as ardently attached to its principles as their brethren." He also stressed to Lafayette that the battlefield ("the ground on which you tread!") served as a "testimonial" to the valor of the Louisiana militiamen.[28] For this reason, the welcome ceremony at the Chalmette Battleground served to legitimize the contribution of Louisiana to the creation and perpetuation of the republic, and in particular the role of the city's Creoles, in a space that evoked memories of their past glory.

During the ceremony at the battleground, Governor Johnson reassured Lafayette that his efforts to bring liberty to his people had not been in vain. Nevertheless, he offered only a tepid appraisal of the Creoles' patriotism and republican sentiment. The Virginia-born Johnson had only recently won the bitter election for governor, during which the Creoles charged the Anglo-Americans with violating a pact stipulating that the position rotate between the two ethnic populations. Johnson informed Lafayette that the "generous efforts in the cause of freedom have not wholly failed in behalf of those who can boast of the same origin with you." He continued with the more gracious observation that "this State settled by Frenchmen, and principally inhabited by their descendents, enjoys as a member of the American confederacy the full measure of their liberty, for which you toiled and bled." Nevertheless, he finished his appraisal by needlessly referencing recent attacks upon their commitment to its liberties, asserting that the "wise and temporate [*sic*] use which Frenchmen have here made of it, is a triumphant answer to those who have proclaimed them unfit for freedom."[29] Lafayette replied that he was "particularly obliged to your friendly and liberal observation, that in this State a daily evidence is given of the fitness of a French population for a wise use

26. A Citizen of New Orleans, 34-35.

27. *Courier*, April 13, 1825, reprinted in Brandon, ed., 166.

28. Ibid.

29. A Citizen of New Orleans, 35.

of the blessings of free institutions, and free government."[30]

The Louisiana militia companies stood at attention throughout the governor's speech. It was well known that Lafayette admired the state militias as protectors of national liberty and sought to encourage European nations to adopt a similar system.[31] For this reason, members of the militia felt a particular pride in meeting Lafayette on the battleground. Their presence at the ceremony, however, was accepted only reluctantly by city leaders. In fact, a resolution submitted to the City Council authorizing the militia to be reviewed by the General was initially rejected.[32] Affrays had been erupting for years between members of the Anglo-American companies and those of the Louisiana Legion, historically dominated by Creoles.[33] Questions over the national status of the Louisiana Legion's membership, for example, began to brew in 1822, when Anglo-Americans charged that it was composed of numerous "Foreign French," a reference to the French nationals immigrating to the city. Complaints by Anglo-Americans reached their height in December 1822 when Major Pierre A. Cuvillier was elected to lead the Legion. Cuvillier, a French national, had not only failed to begin the naturalization process, but had also fought alongside the British during the American Revolution. This prompted the Anglo-American press to disparage the thought of the militia taking orders from "vile mercenary wretches."[34] The controversy did not end in time for the eighth of January celebration in 1823 when the Anglo-American militia, the Louisiana Guards, refused to march in the procession alongside the Legion.[35] The Fourth of July celebration of 1824 similarly provoked heated anger. Seven months earlier, the legislature had designated William L. Robeson, an Anglo-American, to be brigadier general of the First Brigade, a move that incensed Creole members of the militia who refused to follow his orders. In retaliation, the Creole leaders in the city ordered Major Bartholomew Grima, of the Creole militia, to lead the legion in the Independence Day parade. This decision led many Anglo-Americans

30. Ibid., 37.

31. Kramer, 205.

32. City Council, *Official Proceedings* (translations), vol. 4, bk. 2, August 18, 1824, NOPL.

33. Fossier, 196-97.

34. Quoted in Tregle, *Louisiana in the Age of Jackson*, 92-93, quotation 93.

35. *Louisiana Gazette*, January 10, 11, 1823; Tregle, *Louisiana in the Age of Jackson*, 93; The militia companies often refused to participate in the ceremonies at all, lest they be forced to ride alongside members of the other companies. Fossier, 486.

to suspect that a foreign faction wished to wrest control of the city. It also sparked some of the first calls for a separation of the city, a threat that would be realized only eleven years later when it separated into three municipalities corresponding to the city's major ethnic factions.[36] When Lafayette arrived in the United States in August 1825, he was informed of the recent controversies in New Orleans, but his attempts to intervene ultimately failed to temper the dispute.[37]

Controversies among the militia, in fact, continued as Lafayette entered the city, which was to be announced by the firing of a salute of one hundred guns. Anglo and Creole superior officers began to bicker over who should have the honor of giving the order, ultimately delaying the salute. At the last possible moment, the Creole commander of the Legion's artillery stepped forward. This move so upset an Anglo officer that he challenged the Creole commander to a duel to take place after Lafayette's departure.[38] Further controversy erupted when the militia units began to fight over who should have the honor of being first to receive Lafayette, the Legion, operated by the Creoles, or the Anglo-American militia. While Lafayette's intervention helped quell the animosities and averted the duel, the unity of the militia proved to be short-lived.[39] Anglo-Americans continued to complain that unnaturalized citizens of foreign descent led the Louisiana Legion.[40]

The welcoming reception offered to Lafayette as he entered the city on April 10, 1824, outshone even Jackson's ceremony in 1815.[41] The people of New Orleans constructed a sixty-eight-foot arch with an entryway forty-feet

36. The city divided into three separate municipalities in 1836. The First Municipality, located roughly within the original city boundaries, contained the French-speaking Creoles. The Second Municipality, located above the First Municipality and containing the Faubourg St. Mary, included many of the Anglo-American migrants. The Third, located below the city in the former Faubourg Marigny, was composed of a mixture of French-speaking Creoles and recently arrived European immigrants.

37. Tregle, *Louisiana in the Age of Jackson*, 95.

38. A. Levasseur, *Lafayette en Amérique, en 1824 et 1825, ou Journal d'un Voyage aux États-Unis*, vol. 2 (Paris: A La Librairie Baudouin, 1829), 218-20; A Citizen of New Orleans, 34.

39. Jane Bacon MacIntire, *Lafayette, The Guest of the Nation: The Tracing of the Route of Lafayette's Tour of the United States in 1824-25* (Newton, MA: The Anthony J. Simone Press, 1967), 168; A Citizen of New Orleans, 81.

40. Tregle, *Louisiana in the Age of Jackson*, 95.

41. *Courier*, April 11, 1825, reprinted in Brandon, ed., 165.

tall. With a twenty-foot passageway, it made an imposing impression in the Place d'Armes, which was once again chosen as the main site for the spectacle. The arch contained twenty-four stones, representing each state of the union. Rising on either side of the arch were allegorical figures of Liberty and Justice, while above them streamers with the words "Washington" and "Lafayette" flew in the breeze. On top of the arch stood a figure representing "Wisdom" with her hand on the bust of Benjamin Franklin. The dedication, "A grateful Republic has erected this Monument to Lafayette," appeared on either side of the entranceway in both French and English, a dual-language practice common during civic celebrations staged by the city.[42]

As Lafayette stepped from the arch with Governor Johnson and the former Creole governor, General Villeré, supporting him, he was greeted by "the venerable Father Antonio de Sedella, curate of the parish of Orleans, at the head of the clergy."[43] Certainly, for this ceremony, the Cathedral and the Catholic faith took center stage, reflecting the continuing presence and power of the Catholic Church and the shared faith of Lafayette. At a time when numerous Anglo residents and travelers disparaged the city's practice of violating the Sabbath, the Creoles of New Orleans proudly pointed to the fact that Lafayette shared their affinity for treating Sunday as a day of relaxation and pleasure. As Patricia Brady points out, New Orleans was a predominantly "Catholic" city, which suited Lafayette's schedule and habits. In other parts of the nation where American Protestants condemned Sabbath activity, Lafayette not only acquiesced in these strictures, but also "allowed his hosts to believe that he shared their sabbatarian views."[44] Once in New Orleans, however, no such issues impeded his travels or activities.

During the ceremony and throughout Lafayette's visit, Creole political leaders and citizens appropriated Lafayette as their brother, forging their own link to the American Revolution and reaffirming their ethnic, religious, and transatlantic loyalties. The Recorder of the City Council, for example, pointed to their shared ancestry, suggesting that as Americans they shared many of the same joys as those in the eastern states, but that "as the descendents of Frenchmen, a natural inclination interests them more directly in every thing

42. It was common for the Declaration of Independence to be read in both English and French during the Fourth of July ceremonies. Fossier, 486; A Citizen of New Orleans, 38-39.

43. A Citizen of New Orleans, 38-39.

44. Brady, 34.

which concerns your glory."[45] Unlike other cities, which might have focused on American traditions and institutions, New Orleans focused on their common cultural ties. As the mayor remarked, "Within these walls erected by our common ancestors, every thing must be for you, General, a source of pleasing emotion. During the too short time you intend to remain among us, you will remark, no doubt, the effects produced by our wise institutions."[46] Despite the increasing number of Anglo-American emigrants from the east, the ceremony emphasized French heritage and the unique melding of French tradition with American identity.

Anglo-American residents, in contrast, attempted to accentuate their distinctly "American" values and contributions during the visit. For these more recent immigrants to the city, the Catholic rituals, foreign languages, and European manners of the Latin Creoles appeared decidedly un-American, and even hostile to the nation's traditions and values. It is likely that many of these recent migrants to the city could trace their own heritage and ancestry to the Revolution. Certainly, their presence in the city helped spark the annual Fourth of July celebrations. Despite their efforts, however, these celebrations could not compete with the eighth of January celebrations dominated by Creoles, for practical as well as civic reasons. The state legislature required elections to begin on the first Monday every July and last for three days, a time frame that often conflicted with Independence Day celebrations. This law led some Anglo-Americans in other parts of the country to speculate that the people of Louisiana were ungrateful for their freedoms and "unworthy of enjoying the fruits of that Liberty." A local Anglo-American editor responded defensively to this charge, arguing that far from making the politicians and citizens unworthy, the people of New Orleans "do every thing after the Northern fashion."[47] At least, he could argue, recent migrants from the North tried to do so.

The controversies that erupted during the initial reception of Lafayette did not subside during his visit. Anglo-Americans and Creoles continued to vie for his attention and demonstrate their distinct contributions to the city and the country. Not surprisingly, the Creoles invited Lafayette to the Orleans Theatre, the pride of their community that signified their French culture and distinguished taste. As the mayor indicated, it was at the French theatre that "New Orleans can seem great, and is in fact, even in the eyes

45. A Citizen of New Orleans, 41-42.

46. Ibid., 40.

47. *Courier*, July 5, 1826.

of those who have visited the Capitals of the North."[48] Anglo-Americans, however, sought to compete with the Latin Creoles for the Marquis's attention by drawing him away from the "French" theater and bringing him to the recently constructed "American" theatre. When the members of the Creole populace discovered that the General intended to visit the American theatre, "the vexation that was felt was not disguised." Only a reassurance that he would attend the Orleans Theatre afterwards calmed the angry citizens, who realized that Lafayette had "condescendingly followed the impulse given him by the Committee of Arrangement."[49]

Upon his arrival at the Anglo-American theater, located in the recently expanded "American" section of the city, or the Faubourg St. Mary, Lafayette received a thunderous welcome that drowned out the performance on stage. One observer noted that this mattered little, for the American performance was "inconsistent." At nine o'clock, two hours later, Lafayette left the American theatre to go to the Orleans Theatre, where the audience welcomed him with applause and cries of "*vive La Fayette*." According to the same citizen who criticized the performance at the American theatre, this performance was "remarkable," with "handsome pieces of poetry" and music by "an amiable and excellent musician." The members of the audience took pride in offering hospitality and honor in a "city that was to show him once again Frenchmen enjoying liberty!"[50] It was proudly noted that the following evening Lafayette once again went to the Orleans Theatre where a special performance of the short variety piece "La Fayette in New Orleans," written for the occasion, honored the General's visit. During the rest of his stay in the city, Lafayette refrained from accepting invitations to private residences for fear of insulting others, but to the delight of the Creole community he visited the Orleans Theatre once more to attend a ball given in his honor.[51]

***

The controversies discussed thus far centered on the cultural and political battles between Anglo-American migrants and Latin Creoles of the city. Although the white men in these groups differed in ethnicity, they could nevertheless claim an equal status as white American nationals. Similarly, race guaranteed a privileged relationship to American national identity for other

48. New Orleans City Council, *Messages from the Mayor* (translations), January 26, 1825, NOPL.

49. A Citizen of New Orleans, 47.

50. Ibid., 47.

51. A Citizen of New Orleans, 52-55, 73.

groups in the city who met with Lafayette, such as the firemen, the Masons, and the members of the Louisiana Bar.[52] It is significant, therefore, that two groups typically excluded from the civic ceremonies of the day, including free people of color and Choctaw Indians, also demanded a voice and sought an audience with Lafayette.

The meeting with the free militia of color and the procession of Choctaw Indian warriors made Lafayette's visit the most inclusive public ceremony in the city during the antebellum era. An analysis of each group's role not only reveals their demand for public power but also highlights their relationship with the nation and the larger Atlantic world. These Americans had fought for the nation to preserve its liberties, fully expecting that, in turn, these liberties would be rightfully bestowed upon them. Instead, both groups found themselves disenfranchised and increasingly denigrated. While both groups wished to thank the General for his service to the country, it is possible that they also sought to symbolically highlight the discrepancy between the ideals of the founders and the realities of contemporary national and local policy. It was well known that Lafayette had spoken out for the liberation of slaves and the equal rights of African Americans. During his tour of the states, furthermore, he made a number of references to the role slaves and free African Americans had played in the Revolutionary victory, statements that local newspapers tended to ignore. He also went out of his way to visit Native American groups and express sympathy with them concerning the increasing encroachment of Euro-Americans on their land.[53] It was not surprising, therefore, that the Creoles of color in New Orleans and the Choctaw Indians believed they would receive a welcome reception from the General.

In a startling display, never duplicated in the civic marches of New Orleans, one hundred Choctaw men, marching silently in single file, followed the Louisiana Legion and other militia groups during the initial public procession into the city. Having fought alongside the United States in the Seminole War, they had camped in the city for almost a month to see "the Great Warrior, Brother of the Great Father Washington." Lafayette received the line of Choctaws and "appeared touched to see that, by a delicate attention, he was informed that his name was known to the warriors of the most retired

52. The General, for example, met with members of the Masons and the Bar Association. Almost three hundred members of the Grand Lodge attended the celebration, where numerous toasts honored the General. More significant, however, was the cultural respect granted to Lafayette by the Most Worshipful Grand Master, Brother Holland. Ibid., 64-71; *Courier*, April 15, 21, 1825; Brandon, ed., 184-92.

53. Kramer, 218-19.

nations."[54] The presence of these warriors did not arouse much comment from the newspapers. Significantly, however, Lafayette's assistant made special note of it.

The other notable group, the "Free Colored Veterans," did not participate in the military review, but did demand a reception with the General during his visit. These men, most of whom were Creoles of distinction, fought honorably during the War of 1812, but had received neither the accolades nor the pensions they had earned. As a result, the group had been "scattered until now."[55] For them, the reception with the General provided the opportunity to share their own melded cultural heritage with Lafayette and receive honors from a man notoriously supportive of the rights of free people of color. The governor did not, however, state this as his main objective for allowing the reception to proceed. According to one witness, he "felt that a patriot so distinguished as La Fayette, would see with pleasure a population of colour, free, obedient to the laws, marching with rapid strides to civilization: and that he would not disdain the homage of those who had spilt their blood in defence [*sic*] of the country." Such a tepid honor illustrates the increasing loss of power experienced by the free militia of color in the city, even as their perseverance illustrated their continued efforts to be recognized as citizens of the nation.[56] Lafayette greeted each member of the delegation individually

54. Levasseur, 210; MacIntire, 167; A Citizen of New Orleans, 42-43.

55. Mr. Mercier, quoted in A Citizen of New Orleans, 60; For more information about free militias of color in New Orleans and of the experiences of Creoles of color and Creole slaves in the early nineteenth century, see Marcus Christian, *Negro Soldiers in the Battle of New Orleans* (New Orleans: The Battle of New Orleans 150th Anniversary Committee of Louisiana, 1965); Albert Thrasher, *On to New Orleans: Louisiana's Heroic 1811 Slave Revolt: A Brief History and Documents Related to the Rising of Slaves in January 1811, in the Territory of New Orleans* (New Orleans: Cypress Press, 1995); Roland McConnell, *Negro Troops of Antebellum Louisiana: A History of the Battalion of Free People of Color* (Baton Rouge: Louisiana State University Press, 1968); Rosemarie Fay Loomis, *Negro Soldiers, Free Men of Color in the Battle of New Orleans, War of 1812* (New Orleans: Aux Quartres Vents, 1991); Donald E. Everett, "Free Persons of Color in New Orleans, 1803-1865" (Ph.D. diss., Tulane University, 1952); Rodolphe Lucien Desdunes, *Our People and Our History: Fifty Creole Portraits*, translated and edited by Sister Dorothea Olga McCants (Baton Rouge: Louisiana State University Press, 1973); Carolyn Cossé Bell, *Revolution, Romanticism, and the Afro-Creole Protest Tradition in Louisiana, 1718-1868* (Baton Rouge: Louisiana State University Press, 1997), especially 52-54.

56. Two white men, Captain Louis Simon and Mr. Mercier, spoke on the veteran's behalf. A Citizen of New Orleans, 60-62, quotation 60; Brandon, ed., 181-82.

and warmly praised their service during the War of 1812. He acknowledged their "valor" and stated that he had "seen African blood shed with honor in our ranks for the cause of the United States."[57] Free Creoles of color would increasingly find their rights stripped away in the decades before the Civil War.[58] During the visit of Lafayette, however, they reaffirmed their roles in shaping the history of the nation and their connection with the hero and redefined, if only for a moment, the spirit of American nationalism.

In contrast to the inclusive presence and voice of men in the ceremonies and receptions honoring Lafayette, women receded into the background during the General's visit. Their silence stands in stark contrast to their role during the celebration of Jackson ten years earlier, when, with the exception of the Abbé Dubourg, they served as the event's main speakers.[59] Determined to demonstrate their equality to Jackson and illuminate their role in the conflict, the men could not put themselves in a position of deference to Jackson, nor thank him for protecting their homes and families. When the women spoke, they offered thanks not only to Jackson but also, and more importantly, to their husbands, brothers, and sons. Fulfilling their roles as grateful republican mothers, sisters, and daughters, these women allowed the men to stand as equals with the American General. As late as 1847, a letter from a woman to her friend confirmed the privileged position women held in this ceremony by indicating that it "sprung from female gratitude, and was arranged entirely by the ladies."[60]

57. Quoted in Kramer, 218.

58. For more information about the struggles of slaves and members of the free community of color in New Orleans in the years preceding the Civil War, see Judith Kelleher Schafer, *Becoming Free, Remaining Free: Manumission and Enslavement in New Orleans, 1846-1862* (Baton Rouge: Louisiana State University Press, 2003).

59. Address of Abbé Dubourg to Jackson, January 23, 1815, in John Brannan, *Official Letters of the Military and Naval Officers of the United States, During the War with Great Britain in the Years 1812, 13, 14, and 15* (Washington: Way and Gideon, 1823.), 467ff.; Response of Jackson to Dubourg, January 23, 1815, in Latour, Appendix XXXV, lxxiii; Eliza Chotard Gould, *Remembrances, 1777-1825*, 20, Manuscript 498, TUSC.

60. *Picayune*, January 8, 1847. The presence and performance of women in Jackson's ceremony has been overlooked by historians of parades and celebrations in the early nineteenth century. Mary Ryan, in her study of civic celebrations in New York, San Francisco, and New Orleans, argues that women first appeared in civic parades in 1842, when they represented the different states of the union in a New York parade. She also asserts that only young boys were allowed to participate in such civic celebrations in the early nineteenth century. Mary Ryan, "The American Parade: Representations of

By 1825, however, women were reduced to a largely emblematic role in the ceremony for Lafayette: seen but not heard and rendered only symbolically in allegorical figures. In this ceremony, men sought to assert their republican manhood through a public display of their gratitude and honor. Women's official spoken participation in the ceremony was confined to the words of an eight-year-old girl, who boarded the ship bearing strawberries and a laurel wreath. She also was the first to speak with Lafayette, reciting a poem that prompted the General to request that she accompany him to the ball in his honor. Soon afterward, Bernard Marigny, a respected Creole who had recently lost the gubernatorial election and who was denied a more prominent role in the ceremony by the City Council, spoke for the ladies in a speech that praised Lafayette's chivalry and honor. Later, when the General entered the city, a group of women stood ready to greet him at the court house.[61] Most of the ladies, however, were confined to waving their handkerchiefs from the balconies, having abandoned their bench seats along the Place d'Armes due to the weather.[62] For free women of color and slave women, even this expression of gratitude was denied. The voice of only one, a free woman of color named Désirée, survives in the records. Désirée wrote a letter to Mayor Roffignac offering her laundering services to the General, declaring that the opportunity to wash his "sacred underdrawers" would "make her happier than the laudresses to Achilles, Hector, Jackson."[63] In spite of the enthusiasm of those like Desirée, such women were relegated to the background and denied a public voice, and found themselves unwelcome within the male sphere of nationalist ritual.

* * *

The sentiments of American liberty and identity expressed in different ways by the diverse residents of New Orleans during the visit of the Marquis de Lafayette demonstrated how each crafted a link between their own history and that of the Revolutionary hero. Throughout his visit, the citizens of New Orleans proved themselves to be worthy patriots, pointing to their defense and bravery in the Battle of New Orleans and their adherence to and celebration of republican institutions in the past decade. As they bid farewell

---

the Nineteenth-Century Social Order," in *The New Cultural History*, ed. Lynn Hunt (Berkeley: University of California Press, 1989), 148.

61. MacIntire, 166; Fossier, 490-91; A Citizen of New Orleans, 34, 37, 40;

62. A Citizen of New Orleans, 41.

63. Mlle. Désirée to Joseph Roffignac, New Orleans, March 19, 1825, Grima Family Papers, HNOC; Brady, 32-33.

to Lafayette, they likely reflected upon the role they would play in continuing his legacy of valor and virtue. The visit prompted some in New Orleans to declare that "it was time to renounce, on the one part and the other, their absurd prejudices, or unjust prepossessions." According to some, even the militiamen felt an overwhelming unity of spirit, as "every trace of division . . . disappeared from among the brave."[64]

In New Orleans, as in many cities across the United States, it was hoped that Lafayette's visit would foster mutual respect among citizens, ease the political factions erupting from the 1824 elections, and promote a nostalgic, romanticized image of the Revolution. Such romantic sentiments, however, could not ease the ethnic and racial tensions that shaped social and political life in New Orleans, and which continued to influence the annual civic celebrations of republican virtue. Only a few months after Lafayette's visit, a man who claimed to represent the "respectable Americans" of the Faubourg St. Mary argued that a city where the English language was "prescribed" and where Anglo-Americans were considered "intriguers" was destined to separate into factions.[65] Such sentiment continued into 1826 when the *Louisiana Gazette*, considered the voice of the Anglo-Americans, reported that the city was "opposing and depressing every thing American." Indeed, they insinuated that the Creole's idea of liberty was "imbibed from the monarchial institution from whence they emigrated."[66] It mattered little to these writers that most Creoles had inhabited the region long before many Anglo-Americans arrived, fought in the Battle of New Orleans, and had recently celebrated their "American identity" with a true hero of the Revolution. As more "Foreign French" arrived in the city, content to retain their customs and socialize with the Creoles, Anglo-Americans felt increasingly threatened and intimidated. Even the Marquis de Lafayette could not completely quell the animosity that characterized relations in the city. By 1832, a group of Anglo-Americans met to call for the formal separation of the Faubourg St. Mary from the rest of the city, a plan that would be implemented a few years later when the city formally divided into three separate municipalities representing Anglo, Creole, and "immigrant" affiliations.[67]

The legacy of the Marquis de Lafayette nevertheless became cemented in both the memories of the city's inhabitants and in the city's landscape. The

64. A Citizen of New Orleans, 81.

65. *Louisiana Gazette*, June 30, 1825.

66. Ibid., January 7, 1826; January 12, 1826.

67. Ibid., December 11, 1832.

decision to name the central square in the second municipality after Lafayette became a means for the city's Anglo-American migrants to symbolically link the hero of the Revolution to their own past. The irony that this hero was a French national could not have been lost on their Creole rivals in the first municipality. In a further ironic twist, the Creoles found their own means to link their historical valor with their patriotism by naming their square after Andrew Jackson, the other "hero" of New Orleans. When this occurred in 1851, however, few mentioned that it was Jackson who had first questioned their honor and patriotism.

For the people of New Orleans, the visit of Lafayette provoked a public debate over the meaning of American identity. It also became the stage upon which men of all races and ethnicities could stake a claim to the nation's history and future. As they shared in the celebration of Lafayette with others in the nation, they also crafted their own distinct narratives that would continue to shape political and cultural life in the coming decades.

3 Lafayette and the Fall of the French Monarchy

Sylvia Neely

Lafayette returned to France after fighting in the American Revolution imbued with a vision of the future for France. He wanted his own country to enjoy the kind of government and society that he had learned to love in the United States. Many thinkers in the late eighteenth century and early nineteenth century thought of the United States as an "infant society" that would eventually grow up to be like Europe. They did not believe that American institutions were relevant for France, and they were more likely to look to Great Britain as a model. Lafayette, however, always expressed an almost visceral hatred of England that stemmed in part from his personal history. His father had been killed in battle fighting the British. But this hatred was also a manifestation of patriotism. He thought the French were better than their English rivals. He had joined the American revolutionaries because he hated Great Britain and because he wanted to contribute to freedom, a term that he used but which lacked specific content for him. America provided the specifics. He determined to devote himself to translating the American experiment in representative institutions into French government and society. Naturally there would have to be some adjustments to make the new political ideas work in France. But he had the ardor of a convert and the courage of a soldier. He was convinced that reform of the monarchical system was possible, and so when the French Revolution began, he plunged into the difficult work of transforming the ancient monarchy into a modern, forward-looking institution. Why did he fail?

It is important to remember that he did fail in France. He may have been given the title the "Hero of Two Worlds," but, in France at least, that title did not survive the French Revolution. In France he was not everybody's hero. In the United States he was universally loved. His triumphal tour of the United States in 1824 has left its mark on our landscape: towns and counties throughout the country are called Fayetteville, Lafayette, or Lagrange (the name of his country estate) and other variants on his name. Why was the young man who was such a resounding success in the American Revolution not able to match that success in France?

Lloyd Kramer has suggested that Lafayette's success during the American Revolution can be attributed to three things. Unlike most Europeans, Lafayette showed respect for Americans, and they appreciated this sentiment, especially coming from a European aristocrat. Second, Lafayette understood that the social system worked differently in America, and he therefore did not expect to be given the same deference in America as noblemen received in Europe. Finally, he understood that revolutionary warfare always had a political component. In order to win a revolution, it was not sufficient to succeed militarily. The army needed the support of the people, and the soldiers expected to be treated as citizens.[1] Why did this young man who had the exquisite tact to succeed in America run into such difficulties in France? This article will explore three ways in which the American Revolution influenced Lafayette and demonstrate why these lessons he learned in America did not translate well into France: public opinion and popularity; law and order; and, finally, war.

PUBLIC OPINION AND POPULARITY

Lafayette was famously criticized for lusting after popularity and fame. Thomas Jefferson, in a much-quoted remark, said that Lafayette's "foible is a canine appetite for popularity and fame." But it is important to see this quote in context because it comes in a paragraph praising Lafayette's accomplishments. Jefferson wrote to Madison in 1787 that Lafayette's

> *zeal* is unbounded, & his *weight* with those in *power, great.* His *education* having been merely *military, commerce* was an unknown field to him. But his good sense enabling him to *comprehend* perfectly whatever is *explained to him, his agency* has been very *efficacious. He* has a great deal of *sound genius,* is well *remarked* by the *King,* & rising in *popularity. He* has nothing against *him, but* the *suspicion* of *republican principles.* I think he will one day *be of* the *ministry.* His foible is, a *canine appetite for popularity and fame;* but he will get *above* this.[2]

1. Presentation by Lloyd Kramer at symposium on "Le Marquis de Lafayette and the Spirit of Revolution," September 26 and 27, 2007 at Meridian International Center, Washington, D. C. See also the first chapter of Lloyd Kramer, *Lafayette in Two Worlds: Public Cultures and Personal Identities in an Age of Revolutions* (Chapel Hill: University of North Carolina Press, 1996), and his essay in this volume.

2. Thomas Jefferson to James Madison, January 30, 1787, in Thomas Jefferson, *The Works of Thomas Jefferson,* Federal Edition (New York and London, G.P. Putnam's Sons,

It is important to remember also that fame to the people of the eighteenth century did not mean the same thing as it does to us in the twenty-first century, when somebody can become a celebrity for behaving badly or for posting a nude video on the Internet. We have learned to be suspicious of mere fame that is created and orchestrated by "the media." The kind of fame the people of the eighteenth century sought was not transient or ephemeral, but would rather be won because the individual had accomplished something great that would live on in the memory of posterity, what the French call "*gloire*."[3] During the French Revolution, Lafayette's enemies accused him of ambition. But, of course, his ambition was not necessarily a bad thing. We need to ask what Lafayette was ambitious for. After all, only ambitious people can do great things. Lafayette was not much different from his contemporaries in his craving for popularity and fame. Long ago, historian Douglass Adair analyzed the ambitions of early Americans in his famous essay entitled "Fame and the Founding Fathers."[4] Frenchmen, too, shared this fascination with fame. The first line of the memoirs of the French revolutionary leader Brissot, who at first sought fame through writing and then through politics, stated: "I loved glory prodigiously."[5]

After the French and American Revolutions inaugurated the era of democratic political systems, in order to accomplish something lasting, a leader needed to rely on popular opinion and support. George Washington understood that concept well and Lafayette always tried to imitate his American mentor. Washington's biographer James Thomas Flexner reminded us that Washington's drive for power and glory derived from Stoic philosophy. Washington was convinced that "the approbation and affections of a free people" were "the greatest of earthly rewards." Washington wrote: "How pitiful in the eyes of reason and ambition is that false ambition which desolates the world with fire and sword for the purposes of conquest and fame, when compared to the milder virtues of making our neighbors and our fellow men

---

1904-5). Vol. 5. Accessed from http://oll.libertyfund.org/title/802/86654 on 2010-01-16. Italicized words were in cipher.

3. Stanley J. Idzerda, "When and Why Lafayette Became a Revolutionary," in *Bourgeois, Sans-Culottes, and Other Frenchmen*, eds. Morris Slavin and Agnes M. Smith (Waterloo, Ontario: Wilfrid Laurier University Press, 1981), 14-16.

4. Douglass Adair, "Fame and the Founding Fathers," in *Fame and the Founding Fathers: Essays by Douglass Adair* (NY: Norton, 1974), 3-26.

5. J.P. Brissot, *Mémoires*, ed. Claude Perroud, 2 vols (Paris: Picard & Fils, 1911), 1:1.

as happy as their frail conditions and perishable natures permit *them to be*."[6]

The nineteen-year-old Lafayette arrived in America thirsting for military glory. He already was convinced that true glory would come by using the sword in a good cause. He wanted to help establish American liberty and save Americans from the tyranny of the British. Americans were happy to have the services of a well-placed French aristocrat and gave him a position on Washington's staff and the rank of major general. In a revealing correspondence with George Washington in December 1777, only six months after arriving in America, the two men showed clearly what they meant by ambition. Lafayette told Washington of his surprise at learning of the schemes of General Conway, an Irish-born soldier and veteran of French service who had enlisted in the American cause. Conway was the center of what is known as the "Conway Cabal" in which Conway hoped to replace Washington at the head of the American army. Having enquired into his character, Lafayette had discovered that he was "an ambitious and dangerous man" who probably "did not do honor" to his country. He confessed that the "gentleman had engaged me by entertaining my head with ideas of glory and shining projects, and I must confess for my shame that it is a too certain way of deceiving me." He promised Washington to serve him loyally and to try "every exertion in my power to succeed."[7] Washington responded that he was pleased to have Lafayette's friendship and was satisfied "that you can have no views to answer by throwing out false colours, and that you possess a Mind too exalted to condescend to dirty arts and low intrigues to acquire a reputation. Happy, thrice happy, would it have been for this Army and the cause we are embarked in, if the same generous spirit had pervaded all the Actors in it." But, he continued, Conway's ambition led him to use disreputable means of gaining position, and he had "practised every art to do me an injury." Washington did not fear public reprobation because "it is well known, that neither ambitious, nor lucrative motives led me to accept my present appointments."[8] Lafayette responded immediately, thanking Washington for his friendship and continuing the discussion of glory by writing (in his still shaky command of the English language), "man do not join the pure ambition of glory with

6. Cited in James Thomas Flexner, *George Washington in the American Revolution (1775-1783)* (Boston: Little, Brown and Company, 1967), 550.

7. Lafayette to George Washington, December 30, 1777, *Lafayette in the Age of the American Revolution: Selected Letters and Papers,* edited by Stanley J. Idzerda, vol. 1 (Ithaca: Cornell University Press, 1977), 205-206. Hereafter cited as *Letters.*

8. Washington to Lafayette, December 31, 1777, *Letters,* 207-208.

the other ambitions of advancement rank and fortune. As an ardent lover of laurels I can not bear the idea that so noble a sentiment should be mixed with Any low one."[9] Glory and lasting fame were Lafayette's goals, but lasting fame, he and his contemporaries believed, could not be attained through base or lowly means.[10] Lafayette learned from Washington that glory was more than military achievement or advancement, and ambition was bad if it was for personal gain only. Many years later, when Lafayette edited his own letters for publication, he omitted that portion in which he confessed to ambition. By then, he had encountered the corrosive criticism of his enemies during the French Revolution who accused him repeatedly of being ambitious and of seeking popularity. As he got older and more experienced, his ambition also matured. He sought glory not for its own sake, but for the sake of accomplishing something lasting for his fellow countrymen and humanity.

During the French Revolution, leadership was automatically suspect. Anybody who worked with the king or who assumed a position of authority was likely to be accused of seeking power for his own sake or of intending to bring back "despotism," as the reign of Louis XVI before the revolution was called. This characteristic of the political culture of the French Revolution seriously undermined the hopes for stability and order. The National Constituent Assembly was so fearful that their leaders would perpetuate themselves in power that (at the instigation of Robespierre) they decreed that none of its members could stand for election to the new Legislative Assembly established by the Constitution of 1791 they had recently written. At a stroke, the most experienced leaders and the men most dedicated to the success of the new Constitution were barred from serving in the new government. If one tried to argue against such an unwise measure, one would be accused of dangerous ambition.[11] The consequences in America would certainly have been markedly different had Washington, Madison, and the other founding fathers been excluded from office after they finished writing the Constitution.

Lafayette had learned in the American Revolution that success depended

9. Lafayette to Washington, December 31, 1777, *Letters*, 209.

10. Adair makes an important distinction between mere success and fame. Adair, "Fame and the Founding Fathers," 7.

11. Barry M. Shapiro, "Self-Sacrifice, Self-Interest, or Self-Defense? The Constituent Assembly and the 'Self-Denying Ordinance' of May 1791," *French Historical Studies,* 25 (Fall 2002): 625-56; Timothy Tackett, "Conspiracy Obsession in a Time of Revolution: French Elites and the Origins of the Terror, 1789–1792," *The American Historical Review,* June 2000 <http://www.historycooperative.org/journals/ahr/105.3/ah000691.html> (July 27, 2010).

on the support of the people. He knew, in other words, that popularity needed to be cultivated and used with care. He tried to teach Louis XVI the rules of this new type of political system. But Louis XVI was not able to learn the lessons that Lafayette had learned from Washington. Louis had been an absolute king who ruled by divine right. He had never had to seek public support. But Louis had nonetheless always tried to consider public opinion, and he began his reign by proclaiming that he wanted to be loved. Lafayette repeatedly urged the king to court popular opinion. It is important to remember that the French Revolution did not begin as an anti-monarchical revolution. There was resentment of the king's government and its policies, but a vast reservoir of goodwill toward the king existed throughout the country. Lafayette hoped to exploit and nurture this goodwill.

In a memorandum to the king on suggestions for future policy, Lafayette insisted that success would come only if the king openly and enthusiastically declared his support for the new order, worked closely with the Assembly, and rallied everybody around "the national banner." The king's role, Lafayette declared, was "to be the man of the people."[12] In May 1790, Lafayette, in another memorandum to the king, insisted on the importance of popularity: ". . . in order to foil the factious, [and] to prevent plots that all good citizens tremble about, the king must not neglect any means of popularity." He recommended that the king review the National Guard troops at the Champ de Mars (the military academy parade grounds) every Sunday. Lafayette suggested abandoning the old rules that stipulated that only nobles of long lineage could appear at court. Such exclusivity bred resentment, he noted. He sent these suggestions in private to the king so that they could remain confidential. Lafayette stressed his devotion, but also his concerns about the future: "Our situation is critical," he wrote.[13]

All of Lafayette's suggestions were for naught. The king suffered from debilitating shyness. He hardly ever traveled. And even though he had been described as an absolutist monarch, Louis's notion of absolutism was that the king should be above all factions and allow his ministers to make all the decisions. In a revolutionary situation, this kind of reticence hurt the royal cause and crippled decisive action. If we could imagine the dynamic and energetic Louis XIV being on the throne at the end of the eighteenth century instead of Louis XVI, we can begin to see the difference that personality can make in

12. *Mémoires, correspondance et manuscrits du général Lafayette, publiés par sa famille,* 6 vols. (Paris: H. Fournier ainé, 1837-1838), II, 437. Hereafter cited as *Mémoires.*

13. Lafayette to Louis XVI, May 26, 1790, *Mémoires*, II, 464-66.

history. Louis XVI had inherited the throne, but he was not well adapted to playing the role of a leader who could take charge during a revolution. British historian Tim Blanning comments on the lost opportunities:

> In the final analysis, it could be said that the constitutional monarchy failed in France because the King declined to play the role allotted to him. This was a personal failure, for on the rare occasions that he managed to speak his lines with conviction, he was almost overwhelmed with the great fund of goodwill towards him which persisted until remarkably late in the day.[14]

Lafayette was delighted when Louis XVI agreed to appear before the Assembly on February 4, 1790, and proclaim his devotion to the constitution that the Assembly was writing. He was greeted by ecstatic acclamations from the deputies. An even more exhilarating experience occurred some five months later on July 14, 1790, at the Fête de la Fédération (the Festival of Federation) on the first anniversary of the fall of the Bastille. Delegations of National Guard troops from throughout the country arrived in Paris for a celebration at the Champ de Mars. The king and his family were there in a special pavilion. The deputies of the Assembly marched in and took their places, as did the ranks of national guardsmen. Lafayette took an oath in the name of the gathered people at the altar of the nation, after which Talleyrand (then a bishop) celebrated a mass. Songs were sung and the crowds were united in a sense of patriotic devotion to the new institutions. Madame de Staël described the scene this way: "M. de La Fayette came up to the . . . altar to swear loyalty to nation, law and king; the oath and the man who pronounced it excited a great feeling of confidence. The spectators were ecstatic; to them king and liberty now seemed completely united."[15] But the occasions on which the king showed his interest in politics of the people or the revolution were few and far between. And Lafayette, conspicuous here at this imposing ceremony, could not take the place of the king as a unifying symbol of the nation.

At the beginning of the revolution, Lafayette had the most authority and popularity, but he was not the king. He was prevented by his disposition, as well, from taking control of events. Lafayette's problem was certainly not shyness. His problem was a devotion to law and order. He wanted the revolution to succeed, but he wanted to stay within the limits of legality. He did

14. Tim Blanning, *The Pursuit of Glory: Europe 1648-1815* (New York: Viking, 2007), 343.

15. Mme de Staël, *Considérations sur la Révolution Française,* edited by the Duc de Broglie and the Baron de Staël (Paris: Delaunay, 1818), 377-78.

not want to take power away from the king or the Assembly. He always kept in mind the principles on which the revolution was based and never wanted to act contrary to those principles. Here again he was imitating George Washington, who always worked with Congress during the Revolution, even though its delays in funding sometimes seemed to threaten the military cause. George Washington recognized that it was not enough to win the war. It had to be won in such a way that a constitutional government that protected liberty would be the result.

LIBERTY AND ORDER

Lafayette occupied a strange position in the French Revolution. He was the symbol of liberty, the hero of two worlds, the man who had first introduced a Declaration of the Rights of Man. But after the fall of the Bastille, he was also essentially the chief of police of the city of Paris. In July 1789, as royal troops were being moved to the area of Paris, supposedly to help keep order in the unruly city, fears spread that the true purpose of the troops was to dissolve the National Assembly and stop the revolution. The government decided that the royal troops were so unreliable that they could not be ordered to put down the disturbances in Paris, and the troops were pulled out of the city. The local authorities then created a local militia to protect the city and maintain order. The crowds that conquered the Bastille were looking for arms for this militia. The fall of the Bastille is so famous because the people of Paris believed that their actions had saved the revolution from the threats of the converging royal troops.

Giving up on the royal government to keep order, the citizens in Paris realized that they would have to provide for the safety of the city themselves. They quickly decided to make their militia of local citizens a permanent institution and asked Lafayette to be the commander. His devotion to revolution was well known. His popularity with the crowds was also obvious. He created a uniform for the National Guard of Paris that used the colors blue, red, and white, which became the national colors of France.[16] But police actions are not often popular, especially in a revolutionary situation. Lafayette believed that if the revolution was to succeed they would need to establish both lib-

16. On Lafayette's role in the events of the early revolution, see Louis Gottschalk and Margaret Maddox, *Lafayette in the French Revolution through the October Days* (Chicago: University of Chicago Press, 1969). On his command of the National Guard of Paris, see Dale Clifford, "The National Guard and the Parisian Community, 1789-90," *French Historical Studies*, 16, no. 4 (Fall 1990), 849-78.

erty and order. He also recognized that his popularity was a valuable asset that he could employ, much like a bank account. He would use some of it for important goals, but at some point, the bank account would be depleted. And that is basically what happened to him during the French Revolution: the bank account of his popularity became depleted because he expended his popularity in trying to establish both liberty and order.

In the first heady days of the summer of 1789, Lafayette's popularity was so great that on several occasions he arrived on the scene and managed to persuade wrought-up crowds to release people they were threatening to lynch. He reported in a letter on July 16, 1789, that he had saved the lives of six individuals "who were being hanged in various neighborhoods."[17] He devoted considerable attention to the reform of the criminal justice system and urged passage of legislation on declaring martial law. He was convinced that disorder was caused not just by the "exaltation of minds going off like volcanoes because of this great revolutionary movement," but that disorders were being "systematically provoked by the party that, profiting from the passions of the moment, and exciting the spirit of brigandage, wanted . . . to prevent the reorganization of France, and destroy and even depopularize liberty by the excesses of licence."[18] Lafayette revealed that he carefully considered what I call the "bank account" of his popularity when he entered into a debate in the Assembly in May 1790 over the role of the king in matters of peace and war. Lafayette sided with Mirabeau in wishing to give more power to the king. However, popular opinion in Paris favored more of a role for the Assembly. Lafayette concluded his speech by saying, "I thought I could not better repay the immense debt that I owe the people, than in not sacrificing to the popularity of a day the opinion that I think is the most useful for it."[19] He would, in other words, sacrifice momentary popularity in order to work for what he believed was in the best interest of the people.

Aware that he was perpetually accused of ambition, Lafayette was careful to point out in his memoirs that he turned down many offers of greater power. The king offered to name him constable of the kingdom. A movement formed among municipal national guards throughout the kingdom to create a unified National Guard for the whole country under his command. Lafayette rejected this idea because he thought it was important for the armed forces to be under the authority of the king. The national guards

17. *Mémoires*, II, 317.

18. Ibid., 378.

19. Ibid., 405.

he envisioned as entirely local organizations of citizens under the control of the civilian municipal authorities.[20]

Lafayette understood the problem of establishing order after a revolution that was necessarily brought about by initial disorder. It is worth considering closely one of the famous quotes from a speech he gave to the National Assembly in early 1790, urging them to complete work on the constitution. The first part of the quotation is well known because it was frequently used by conservatives accusing Lafayette of being a rabble-rouser. Lafayette declared that disorders had been necessary to bring about the revolution and to eliminate the oppression of the old order. In that case, he said, "insurrection is the most sacred of duties." That phrase is well known, but the rest of the quotation emphasizes order rather than revolution: "insurrection is the most sacred of duties but for the constitution, the new order must become stronger, people must be safe, the new constitution must be loved, public power must take on strength and energy."[21] So for Lafayette, the revolution was needed only to bring about liberty and that liberty, once secured, needed to be enshrined in a system of laws (a constitution) and in a government strong enough to make the system of laws obeyed. In November 1789, he wrote to his cousin General Bouillé that although they had disagreed on the means of bringing about liberty, and the amount of it there should be, they could now both agree on what they feared: "anarchy, civil dissensions, the dissolution of all public forces." They both wanted "the reestablishment of credit, the strengthening of constitutional liberty, the return of order, and a strong measure of executive power."[22]

An example of his devotion to law and order that has frequently been misunderstood by historians is his reaction to what one might call the Saint Cloud incident. In the spring of 1791, the king wanted to travel to an estate outside Paris at Saint Cloud to spend Easter. One of the reasons for his trip was religious scruples. The Church had lost its income when the Assembly took over church lands to pay the country's debts and when the system of seigneurial or feudal payments was abolished. In order to support the Church, the Assembly decreed that the state would pay the priests, but they insisted that priests take an oath to the new constitution and to the law. Because the pope had not consented to this change nor had a church council been consulted, some priests refused to take the oath. They became known as "non-

20. *Mémoires*, II, 379-81.

21. Ibid., 383.

22. Lafayette to Bouillé, November 14, 1789, Ibid., 423-24.

juring" priests. Those who did take the oath were called constitutional priests. Louis XVI was a sincere and pious Catholic. He did not want to take his Easter communion in Paris from a constitutional priest. Everybody understood his motives well, but they disagreed on their meaning. Radical revolutionaries in Paris believed the non-juring priests were really counterrevolutionary, that they were using religion as an excuse for a basically political act, rejection of the revolution. Louis, radicals believed, was siding with the enemies of the revolution by choosing a non-juring priest at Easter. Those who supported the non-juring priests believed that the Assembly had overstepped its authority by this religious legislation. They were convinced that the real motive of the revolutionaries was not to provide income for the Church, but rather to destroy the Catholic faith.

When Louis XVI and his family tried to leave the Tuileries Palace on April 17, 1791, to go to Saint Cloud, crowds prevented them from leaving, and the National Guard troops refused to open a way for the king's carriage despite Lafayette's entreaties and express orders to them. The king returned to the palace and gave up the trip. Lafayette was furious at what had occurred and submitted his resignation as commander of the Paris National Guard. The national guardsmen responded by begging him to rescind his resignation. They expressed continued devotion to him and promised to obey in the future. Lafayette did call back his resignation and continued to serve as commander. Here is how one historian, Patrice Gueniffey, interpreted this event:

> . . . twenty-three of the sixty battalions of the National Guard asked him to remain at his post. When he seemed to hesitate, forty battalions approached him again, whereupon Lafayette gave in and withdrew his resignation. Was this simply an emotional reaction? Nothing could be less certain; perhaps he had wished to test the loyalty of his troops, some of whom had failed him on April 17. The trap slammed shut: a general, whose authority derived solely from the law, had accepted a personal oath of allegiance. Indeed, several battalions had sworn "an inviolable oath of loyalty and unlimited confidence" in him and had even expelled those who refused to participate. By not disavowing this plebiscite, Lafayette became its accomplice.[23]

Gueniffey believes that this incident proved that Lafayette intended to create a purely personal following and make himself a dictator.

Lafayette's enemies may have believed that is what he intended, but the actual events and Lafayette's own explanation of them contradict that con-

23. Patrice Gueniffey, "Lafayette," in *A Critical Dictionary of the French Revolution*, eds. François Furet and Mona Ozouf (Cambridge: Harvard University Press, 1989), 230.

clusion. Far from flaunting the law or trying to circumvent it, Lafayette was trying to make the point that laws had to be obeyed. In his statement before the city government explaining his resignation, he denied that he had been motivated by sympathy for the king. He asserted that the National Guard troops could certainly understand the discouragement he felt at seeing

> the constitutional authorities ignored, their orders scorned, the forces of order opposed to the carrying out of the very law whose protection is confided to them. . . . We are citizens, Messieurs, we are free; but without obedience to the law, there is nothing more than confusion, anarchy, despotism; and if this capital, the cradle of the revolution, instead of surrounding the depositaries of the powers of the nation with wisdom and respect, instead assails them with tumults or fatigues them with violence, it [the capital] will cease to be the example for French people, it would risk becoming the terror [of French people].
>
> However, Messieurs, in the very touching marks of affection that I have received, too much has been done for me and not enough for the law.

He went on to say that he could only continue to serve if he were convinced that the troops unanimously believed that the future of the constitution was "attached to the execution of the law, the only sovereign of a free people; that the liberty of individuals, the security of places of residence, religious freedom, [and] respect for legitimate authority would be for them, without exception, as sacred as they are for me."[24]

The sixty battalions of the National Guard passed resolutions promising to obey the law. One of them asserted that "M. de Lafayette ceased to command them only because they ceased obeying the law; he wishes a complete submission to the law and not a servile attachment to his person."[25] All troops were then ordered to gather and take an oath that they would obey the law. Only then did Lafayette reassume his command. Lafayette explained his motives clearly in a letter to George Washington, enclosing the speech he had given. Lafayette said that he "stood alone in defense of the law, and turned the tide up into the Constitutional Channel. I hope this lesson will serve my country, and help towards establishing the principles of good order. But before I could bring my fellow citizens to a sense of legal subordination I must

24. *Mémoires*, III, 68. This speech is also in Sigismond Lacroix, *Actes de la Commune de Paris Pendant la Révolution* (New York: AMS Press, 1974, reprint of original edition of 1905), vol. 3, 725-26. Lacroix provides considerable documentation on these events.

25. *Moniteur Universel* 8, no. 114, April 24, 1791, 202.

have conducted them through the fear to loose [*sic*] the man they love."[26] Once again, then, Lafayette was consciously using his popularity as a way to bring about the kind of liberty and political system that he wanted to establish by persuading the national guardsmen to obey the law. But his enemies chose to see only the appeals to personality and popularity and to ignore the principles that lay behind the actions.

Lafayette's role as chief policeman of the city of Paris caused a sharp drop in his popularity at the time of the Flight to Varennes, the king's unsuccessful attempt to flee from Paris in June 1791. Lafayette was placed in grave danger at first because he was falsely suspected of conspiring with the king to allow his escape. Then after the king was stopped at Varennes and returned to Paris, Lafayette was at the head of the National Guard when the municipal authorities ordered them to break up a demonstration at the Champ de Mars. On July 17, a large crowd had gathered to sign a petition asking the Assembly to put the fate of the king up to a vote of the people. But the Assembly had already determined that Louis could remain as king if he accepted the constitution that they were quickly revising and completing. The authorities became increasingly worried at the size of the crowd and feared they would turn even more violent. Two men found hiding under the platform where the petition was being signed had been killed by people who assumed the men were spies or were planting explosives. Most historians, however, believe they had positioned themselves there to look up the skirts of the women as they crossed the platform. When the worried authorities ordered the National Guard to disperse the crowd, violence erupted. Exactly who attacked first is a matter of controversy and how many people died is a matter of debate (perhaps around fifty, though the radicals in Paris said there were hundreds). From that point on, Lafayette's name was inexorably linked to this event, which became known as the Massacre of the Champ de Mars.[27] Radicals in Paris were now completely opposed to Lafayette, believing him to be an accomplice of a king who could no longer be trusted.

Lafayette's involvement in these events demonstrates that while the revolutionaries in Paris were becoming more radical, Lafayette was not. Indeed, he feared that increasing radicalism would threaten the constitutional monarchy that they had been trying to write a constitution for during the previous

26. Lafayette to George Washington, May 3, 1791, *Letters of Lafayette to Washington*, 354.

27. For the events surrounding the Flight to Varennes, see Timothy Tackett, *When the King Took Flight* (Cambridge: Harvard University Press, 2003).

two years. After the Flight to Varennes, he therefore supported putting Louis XVI back on the throne as the first monarch under a constitutional system that finally began in the fall of 1791. The revolution in the strict legal sense was now over. Instead of a revolutionary assembly writing a constitution, there was now a constitutional system with a king and an elected assembly. Lafayette resigned as commander of the National Guard of Paris and moved to his ancestral home at Chavaniac in the Auvergne. The new constitutional government was not destined to last for very long, and one of the reasons that it did not last was the coming of war. Lafayette desperately wanted the constitutional government to survive. Yet he favored the war and became one of the principal generals leading the war. Why did he favor something that destroyed the monarchy?

WAR

In his attitude toward war, we can once again see the influence of Lafayette's experience in America. In America, the Revolutionary War had resulted in the establishment of a constitutional system founded on the sovereignty of the people. It had created the reputation of George Washington, who led the country in war and in peace. Lafayette, then, had learned that a popular military hero could unify the country behind him and create stable institutions. It was, of course, impossible for Lafayette to be the "George Washington" of France, because Lafayette was not the head of state. But he hoped that war would make the king popular and rally the country behind the new constitution. Fighting foreign powers, he believed, would promote nationalism, heal political divisions, and give the government more power to maintain stability.

Lafayette was in favor of war in the spring of 1792 because war offered a way to increase the power of the government. The traditional powers of the king over the army had been curtailed in the summer of 1789 because of fears that the king would use the army to destroy the revolution. The members of the National Assembly had therefore decided that the civil authorities at the local level could request the army to put down civil disturbances or riots, but the king could not deploy the army inside the country in peacetime. According to the Constitution of 1791, the king enjoyed extensive powers when the nation was at war and he commanded the army against foreign aggressors.[28] War, Lafayette and others hoped, would give more power to the

28. John Hall Stewart, *Documentary Survey of the French Revolution* (New York: Macmillan, 1951), 253, 258-59.

king's government, and a more powerful central government might be able to put an end to radical revolutionary demands and stop the revolution.

The main supporter of war was a member of the new Legislative Assembly named Jacques-Pierre Brissot. Brissot's motives were the exact opposite of Lafayette's. Brissot wanted to mount "a crusade of universal freedom."[29] He wished to export freedom to other European countries and to defeat the kings whom he saw as the enemies of the French Revolution. His not so hidden motive was to force Louis XVI to show his true colors. Brissot believed that the king was not genuinely committed to the new constitution and that under conditions of war the king would reveal his treachery, and the revolutionaries would then be justified in getting rid of him. Brissot declared, "the chief executive officer [Louis XVI] will be forced to rule in accordance with the constitution. If he does his duty, we will support him whole-heartedly; but if he betrays us, the people will be ready."[30] Brissot optimistically believed that the war would be short, that French armies would be greeted enthusiastically by the populations in lands subjected to Austrian domination, and that French citizens committed to a cause would naturally prevail over the paid soldiers of the Austrians. So Brissot and Lafayette both favored war, though they favored different kinds of war and for different purposes. Lafayette wanted a short and limited war. Brissot wanted a continent-wide crusade. Brissot wanted to extend the revolution to the rest of Europe; Lafayette wanted to put a halt to it.

Almost alone in opposing war was someone whose later career might make this position seem surprising: Robespierre. He opposed the war because he agreed with Lafayette in thinking that the war would give power to the royal government and to the generals, including Lafayette, whom Robespierre despised and distrusted. He warned Brissot, "You propose to give supreme power to those who most want your ruin."[31] Rejecting the suggestion that people in foreign countries would greet the French as liberators because they would help them throw off their rulers and allow them to adopt the new French institutions, Robespierre reminded those favoring war that "No one loves armed missionaries; and the first counsel that nature and prudence give

29. Quoted in Georges Lefebvre, *The French Revolution from its Origins to 1793*, trans., Elizabeth Moss Evanson (New York: Columbia University Press, 1962), 217.

30. Quoted in M. J. Sydenham, *The French Revolution* (New York: Capricorn Books, 1966), 91.

31. Quoted in Sydenham, *The French Revolution*, 97.

is to repulse them as enemies."[32]

Brissot carried the day. His speeches in favor of war were greeted with raptures of delight as the members of the Legislative Assembly believed their national existence was being threatened and their honor was being insulted. They reacted with nationalistic fervor, and when war was voted only a handful of deputies had the courage to vote no. Brissot turned out to be right in his prediction that the war would bring on the fall of the king. But he was not right in his prediction that the war would be short and victorious and that the people of Europe would welcome the French soldiers with open arms. The war was not short. Once begun in the spring of 1792, it lasted for over twenty-three years until the final defeat of Napoleon.[33]

In December 1791, Lafayette had been named a general of one of the three armies created to defend the country. Lafayette worked hard to get his army in shape, to eliminate officers who were not loyal to the new institutions, and to preserve his army in hopes of using it to protect the king and the constitution. Perhaps again inspired by George Washington, Lafayette favored a defensive posture to keep the poorly organized and undisciplined French army from being utterly defeated. But to radical revolutionaries, defensive measures were signs of lack of devotion to the revolutionary cause. They favored boldness and attack. Anything else seemed proof of treason.

The war began very badly for the French, with a poorly prepared French army marching into the Austrian Netherlands only to retreat ignominiously. One of the generals was lynched because the soldiers believed he had led them into an ambush. Lafayette was appalled at the orders that were coming from Dumouriez, the principal minister in power, who was essentially directing the war effort and often going over the heads of the principal commanders to give orders to their subordinates. And the king, who had not shown much enthusiasm for the war, was immediately suspected of wanting the enemy to win, to march on Paris, and to rescue him. Indeed, Marie Antoinette had been writing letters begging her Austrian relatives to save them, although the people at the time had no way of knowing this for certain.[34]

32. Laura Mason and Tracey Rizzo, *The French Revolution: A Document Collection* (Boston: Houghton Mifflin, 1999), 161.

33. On the coming of war, see T. C. W. Blanning, *The Origins of the French Revolutionary Wars* (London and New York: Longman, 1986).

34. See Munro Price, *The Road from Versailles: Louis XVI, Marie Antoinette, and the Fall of the French Monarchy* (New York: St. Martin's, 2003) for the duplicitous policy of Louis XVI and Marie Antoinette.

So the war, instead of increasing the king's power as Lafayette had hoped, increased suspicions that the king was a traitor and wanted France to lose the war. War was declared in April 1792. The crowds in Paris deposed the king on August 10, 1792.

Lafayette made an effort to undo the Revolution of August 10 by trying to persuade authorities in areas outside of Paris to declare their opposition to it. He hoped that departmental authorities, who were in general less radical than the officials in Paris, would denounce the violence against the king and the National Assembly and thus establish an alternate source of authority in the country. But, with the enemy bearing down on the country, that movement did not go very far. Lafayette soon discovered that his army would not back him up in this scheme. The National Assembly, under the sway of the crowds in Paris, declared Lafayette a traitor and an outlaw. Lafayette left the country, intending to head for Great Britain and perhaps later the United States. To leave the country, however, he had to cross the lines of the invading armies. And when he did so he was captured by the Prussians and Austrians and kept in prison for five long years. To the radical revolutionaries back in Paris, Lafayette was a traitor to the revolution. To the Austrians, he was nothing but a dangerous revolutionary.

So ended (at least temporarily) Lafayette's attempt to translate to France the lessons he had learned in America. The French Revolution became even more violent and radical after the fall of the king, culminating a year later in the Reign of Terror. So why had Lafayette, who as a young man so perceptively found the way to be a great success in the American Revolution, been unable to enjoy the same success in France? Part of the answer may be that early success made him overly optimistic. George Washington's considerable political skills made his accomplishments look easier than they really were. Lafayette perhaps also had too high an opinion of his fellow countrymen. Lafayette, from an ancient noble family, had been able to shed the prejudices of the past and embrace the new ideas of liberty and sovereignty of the people. He was too optimistic that his countrymen could do the same thing. Instead freedom unleashed tensions in society that had been held in check by absolutism. War and civil war fed suspicions of treason and seemed to justify extraordinary measures. Law, order, and constitutionality fell victim to the increasing violence, and so did Lafayette's dreams for establishing liberty and constitutional order in France.

Despite his failure, Lafayette was instrumental in the creation of something very important that survived the revolution: the Declaration of the Rights of Man and Citizen. It inspired people around the world who were embarking on the process of establishing democratic institutions and constitutions. It would become even more significant to people in the twentieth century who witnessed the horrors of genocide. Early in its history, the United Nations responded to human rights violations by publishing a Universal Declaration of Human Rights. On July 11, 1789, even before the fall of the Bastille, when it was not at all clear that the National Assembly would survive, Lafayette introduced his draft of a declaration of rights to the assembly. Lafayette brought it forward at that point because, as he later explained to Thomas Paine, "if the National Assembly should fail in the threatened destruction that then surrounded it, some trace of its principles might have a chance of surviving the wreck."[35] Others contributed to the final version, but much of Lafayette's original draft can be seen in the Declaration of the Rights of Man. He was justly proud of his contribution to this important document. We might see in it one of the most important lessons that Lafayette learned in America. He learned that constitutions and written documents to protect the rights of people were a fundamental part of free governments. Lafayette had difficulty making this vision a reality in France, but his contribution endured to inspire generations long after his death. He would have been pleased because this longevity was, after all, the kind of fame and glory that he sought so avidly throughout his life.

35. Thomas Paine, *Rights of Man*, in *The Complete Writing of Thomas Paine*, ed. P. S. Foner (ed.), (New York, 1945), I, 262.

4 Lafayette, Agent of the "American Mission"

Anne C. Loveland

Many Americans of the late eighteenth and first half of the nineteenth century believed that the United States had a duty to promote liberty and republican government throughout the world. The pre-eminent source of this "American mission" was the Declaration of Independence. In the second paragraph, Thomas Jefferson asserted the "right," even the "duty," of all people (not just British colonists) to "alter" or to "abolish" a government that did not protect and promote their "unalienable rights," which included "life, liberty, and the pursuit of happiness." And, the Declaration continues, their right "to institute new government, laying its foundation on such principles, and organizing its power in such form, as to them shall seem most likely to effect their safety and happiness."[1]

Another component of the American mission was the notion that the Americans provided a model of the kind of revolution and government most likely to secure liberty. They had successfully revolted against British "tyranny," thrown off monarchy, and established a new government in the form of a federal republic. Many late eighteenth and early nineteenth century Americans agreed with Daniel Webster's description of the American Revolution, in his 1825 Bunker Hill Monument address, as "the wonder and the blessing of the world."[2] Equally significant, they also believed that all human beings were capable of instituting and maintaining a republican form of government. For most Americans it was a "one size fits all" model, appropriate to

1. On the "universalistic worldview" of the Declaration of Independence and its influence on the American mission, see Robert Kagan, *Dangerous Nation* (New York: Alfred A. Knopf, 2006), 40-43.

2. Daniel Webster, "The Bunker Hill Monument" (address delivered at the laying of the cornerstone of the Bunker Hill Monument, Charlestown, Massachusetts, June 17, 1825), in *The Speeches of Daniel Webster*, ed. Rev. B. F. Tefft (New York: The Chesterfield Society, n.d.), 167.

all peoples, climes and conditions, guaranteed to produce safety and happiness wherever instituted.

In the late eighteenth and early nineteenth century Americans regarded the Marquis de Lafayette as the agent of the American mission. He was the individual they most trusted to promote the cause of liberty and republicanism throughout the world. As Lloyd Kramer points out in *Lafayette in Two Worlds*, the Marquis was quite aware of the importance of symbolism in political life, and he frequently engaged in symbolic actions affirming his role as agent of the American mission. For example, after the storming of the Bastille, he sent George Washington the key to the prison. In the letter that accompanied the key, he wrote, "It is a tribute which I owe as a son to my adoptive father, as an aid [*sic*] de camp to my general, as a Missionary of Liberty to its Patriarch."[3] Lafayette was not alone in appreciating the importance of symbolism. Thomas Paine, who conveyed Lafayette's memento to Washington, reinforced its symbolic meaning by observing that "the principles of America opened the Bastille . . . and therefore the Key comes to the right place." And Washington wrote to Lafayette that he accepted the key as "the token of victory by Liberty over Despotism."[4]

Another symbolic action Lafayette used to fashion his image as agent of the American mission was participation in annual Fourth of July celebrations in Paris, which were faithfully reported by U.S. newspapers. Here is a toast he gave on one such occasion: "American liberty, founded on the rights of men and nations; may this doctrine open all eyes, fortify every arm, and may the cause of Europe triumph over the late convulsions of despotism and privilege."[5]

Most historians today would agree that Lafayette was not just playing a role, that he really believed in the American mission. Throughout his career he demonstrated devotion to the principles and values he had learned in America during the War for Independence. He consistently championed the

3. Lloyd Kramer, *Lafayette in Two Worlds: Public Cultures and Personal Identities in an Age of Revolutions* (Chapel Hill: University of North Carolina Press, 1996), 32, 35.

4. Thomas Paine to Washington, May 1, 1790, in Moncure D. Conway, *The Life of Thomas Paine: With a History of His Literary, Political and Religious Career in America, France, and England* (New York: G. P. Putnam's Sons, 1892), I: 273; Washington to Lafayette, August 11, 1790, in *The Writings of George Washington from the Original Manuscript Sources, 1745-1799*, ed. John C. Fitzpatrick (Washington: Government Printing Office, 1931-44), XXXI: 85-86.

5. *Niles' Weekly Register* (Baltimore), September 22, 1821, p. 61, and see also August 30, 1823, p. 410.

inalienable rights of man, and, perhaps even more importantly, lauded the American example.[6] In a farewell address he delivered at the end of his visit to the United States in 1784, he saluted the nation as an "immense temple of freedom . . . a lesson to oppressors, an example to the oppressed, a sanctuary for the rights of mankind."[7] In 1832, in a speech to the French Chamber of Deputies, he called the government of the United States "the *pattern Government*" and declared that "republican institutions . . . are suited to every country where the citizens are intelligent, and wish to be free."[8] For Americans, he remained an ideological certainty amidst the confusing complexities of European politics.

In the Arthur H. and Mary Marden Dean Lafayette Collection at Cornell University are hundreds of letters Americans wrote to Lafayette during the late eighteenth and early nineteenth century. Some of the writers were government officials or members of the intellectual or economic elite in the United States, but a considerable number were ordinary citizens. Many of them wrote to him expressing their hopes for the cause of liberty in Europe or offering their assessments of political conditions in that part of the world. Lafayette called these advocates of the American mission "the friends of liberty."

Three revolutions in Europe engaged Lafayette and the American friends of liberty. Their voluminous correspondence gives a good idea of the ways in which Lafayette really did and did not play the role of agent of the American mission in these revolutions and how his American friends responded to his actions and to the course the revolutions followed. Each of them provided a testing ground for the American mission, forcing Americans to ponder its meaning and implications. As we shall see, some Americans questioned or even revised the American mission, while others continued to accept and believe in it as originally formulated. The American response to the three revolutions also exhibits a definite pattern. Initially, when Americans first heard the news of the outbreak of the revolutions, they expressed great en-

6. Kramer, *Lafayette in Two Worlds*, 34, 35-37, 43, 52.

7. *Journals of the Continental Congress, 1774-1789*, ed. Worthington Chauncey Ford (Washington: Government Printing Office, 1904-1937), XXVII: 684 (December 13, 1784). According to Louis R. Gottschalk, *Lafayette Between the American and the French Revolution, 1783-1789* (Chicago: University of Chicago Press, 1950), 137, the farewell address was published in full in many American newspapers.

8. Philadelphia *National Gazette*, March 21, 1833; Washington *Daily National Intelligencer*, March 25, 1833.

thusiasm and optimism. But as the revolutions proceeded, such sentiments soon gave way to skepticism, disillusionment, and even despair.

The French Revolution of 1789

When news of the outbreak of the French Revolution reached the United States, Americans congratulated themselves on the salutary effect of the American example. They credited the Marquis de Lafayette and other French officers who had served in the American Revolution with having transported "American principles" to their native land.[9] Much of the enthusiasm Americans felt for the revolution derived from the belief that Lafayette was leading it. His eventual fall from power planted seeds of doubt that blossomed into widespread disenchantment. According to the American view, what began as a revolution for liberty, based on the American example and led by America's adopted son, had degenerated into the tyranny of party spirit and mob rule. Lafayette, "the true friend of rational liberty," had become "the unfortunate victim of anarchy and despotism."[10]

The 1789 revolution proved to be a chastening experience for Americans. It shook their confidence that American principles could be transplanted intact to the rest of the world, and that once transplanted they would produce civil order and political moderation, just as they had in the United States. The later phases of the revolution suggested that the soil of the Old World was very different from that of the New and that the tree of liberty would have a more difficult time taking root there than it had in the United States. Reluctantly, some Americans conceded that the planting and cultivation of republican principles in the Old World would necessarily be a slow and gradual process.

Such thoughts Thomas Jefferson expressed in a letter to Lafayette in 1815. Initially, Jefferson had been an ardent supporter of the French Revolution, but like many other Americans had ultimately become disillusioned by its excesses and by the political embarrassment it caused him in the United States. Now he cautioned Lafayette that "a full measure of liberty is not now perhaps to be expected by your nation, nor am I confident they are prepared

9. *Pennsylvania Packet* (Philadelphia), October 16, December 1, 1789; Thomas Jefferson to Dr. Richard Price, January 8, 1789, in *The Life and Selected Writings of Thomas Jefferson*, ed. Adrienne Koch and William Peden (New York: Random House, 1944), 453-54; Thomas Paine, *Rights of Man* (1791), in *The Writings of Thomas Paine*, ed. Moncure Daniel Conway (New York: G. P. Putnam's Sons, 1894-96), II: 336, 355-56.

10. *Connecticut Courant* (Hartford), July 7, 1794, May 8, 1797.

to preserve it." Jefferson estimated that it would take "more than a generation" before the people of France "will be capable of estimating the value of freedom, and the necessity of a sacred adherence to the principles on which it rests for preservation." That capability would come only with "the progress of knowledge in the general mass of the people, and their habituation to an independent security of person and property."[11] Jefferson seemed to be saying that a people's ability to sustain liberty and republican institutions depends on their history and on prevailing social, economic, and political conditions. The extension of "American principles" may happen more quickly and with less trauma in some countries than in others. Different peoples have different tolerances for liberty and republican institutions. If they are not prepared for them, their revolution may degenerate into tyranny, as the French Revolution of 1789 did, or, alternatively, into anarchy.

THE GREEK REVOLUTION OF 1821-1830

The American response to the Greek revolution reveals a pattern similar to the reaction to the French Revolution of 1789. The Greeks had suffered under the domination of the Ottoman Empire since 1460, and the news of their uprising against the Turks in 1821, which was reported in U.S. newspapers, generated great sympathy among the American people during the mid 1820s.[12]

Lafayette was also sympathetic to the Greek cause.[13] He met with several Greeks involved in the revolution and introduced two of them to Albert Gallatin, the U.S. ambassador to France.[14] In 1822 he began sending letters about the Greeks to prominent political leaders in the United States: Thomas Jefferson, John Quincy Adams, William Crawford, Henry Clay, and the President of the United States, James Monroe.[15] The attitude of the

11. Jefferson to Lafayette, February 14, 1815, in *The Works of Thomas Jefferson*, ed. Paul Leicester Ford (New York: G. P. Putnam's Sons, 1904-1905), XI: 454-58.

12. The most complete discussion of "the Greek fever" may be found in Stephen A. Larrabee, *Hellas Observed: The American Experience of Greece, 1775-1865* (Washington Square, NY: New York University Press, 1957) chaps. 3-7.

13. Sylvia Neely, *Lafayette and the Liberal Ideal, 1814-1824: Politics and Conspiracy in an Age of Reaction* (Carbondale: Southern Illinois University Press, 1991), 165, 174; Kramer, *Lafayette in Two Worlds*, 105.

14. Neely, *Lafayette and the Liberal Ideal*, 240.

15. Kramer, *Lafayette in Two Worlds*, 106.

European powers was "unfeeling" and "selfish," he explained to Monroe in 1822; only to the United States could the Greeks look for "honest and efficient support."[16] Lafayette wanted the U.S. government to aid them by sending a naval squadron to the Mediterranean and by loaning them money. "A few friendly ships, a trifling loan of money would render them immense service," he wrote to the President.[17] Several months later he elaborated on his request in a letter to Henry Clay:

> How happy should I be to see an American squadron in those seas! The American flag should be the natural, disinterested protector for the Grecian confederacy. Should the Ottoman navy prove impertinent, it might be crushed at once. A Grecian citizen . . . tells me that two millions of dollars, two ships of the line, or three or four large frigates, could they obtain that sum and naval means from mercantile enterprise, would suffice to insure the liberties of that classic country.[18]

Lafayette's appeals for U.S. aid to the Greeks fell on mostly deaf ears. President Monroe briefly considered helping the Greeks but changed his mind; in the Monroe Doctrine of 1823 he promised that the United States would not interfere in European affairs, if the European nations refrained from interference in the American hemisphere.[19] Other American political leaders Lafayette petitioned for aid to the Greeks agreed with the government's policy of non-involvement. Except Albert Gallatin. Expressing unbounded enthusiasm for the Greek cause, he portrayed it as a momentous struggle "of the civilized world against barbarism, of Christianity against the intolerance of fanaticism, of liberty against tyranny, and of national independence against foreign usurpation."[20] Gallatin strongly supported Lafayette's pleas for a U.S. naval intervention.[21]

16. Lafayette to Monroe, January 22, 1822, quoted in Neely, *Lafayette and the Liberal Ideal*, 241.

17. Lafayette to Monroe, July 13, 1822, quoted in ibid., 241.

18. Lafayette to Clay, November 5, 1822, in *The Life, Correspondence, and Speeches of Henry Clay*, ed. Calvin Colton (New York: P. O'Shea, 1864), IV: 68.

19. Neely, *Lafayette and the Liberal Ideal*, 153. For a more elaborate discussion of why most American political leaders favored non-involvement in the Greek revolution, see Kramer, *Lafayette in Two Worlds*, 105-106.

20. Gallatin quoted in Neely, *Lafayette and the Liberal Ideal*, 240.

21. Larrabee, *Hellas Observed*, 65-74.

While Lafayette's appeals to American political leaders failed to produce the U.S. government action he desired, he achieved more success in arousing support for the Greeks among the American people during his Triumphal Tour of the United States in 1824-1825. Wherever possible, at banquets, receptions, and other public celebrations held in his honor, Lafayette and other advocates of the Greek cause called attention to the Greek people and their revolution. They reminded the American people of the "glories" of ancient Greece and the "splendor and renown" of Athens and Sparta.[22] They pointed out similarities between the Greeks' struggle for liberty against the Turks and the Americans' struggle against British tyranny.[23] On the occasion of Lafayette's visit to Uniontown, Pennsylvania, Gallatin made an impassioned appeal for U.S. intervention. "The cause is not yet won," he cried. "An almost miraculous resistance may yet perhaps be overwhelmed by the tremendous superiority of numbers. And will the civilized, the christian [*sic*] world . . . look with apathy on the dreadful catastrophe that would ensue? a catastrophe which they, which even we alone could prevent with so much facility and almost without danger?"[24]

Few speakers who declared their sympathy for the Greeks during Lafayette's tour went as far as Gallatin did in advocating U.S. government intervention. They believed the United States should limit its support for Greece to "moral influence." In his address at the laying of the cornerstone of the Bunker Hill Monument, Daniel Webster advocated government non-involvement in the Greek revolution at the same time that he urged the American people to encourage Greece in her struggle for independence. "Let her be assured, that she is not forgotten in the world; that her efforts are applauded, and that constant prayers ascend for her success," he declared.[25]

During Lafayette's tour, some speakers urged individual Americans to act in support of the Greek revolution. They presented the example of Lafay-

22. Toast at banquet for Lafayette in Washington, D. C., quoted in Kramer, 107, *Lafayette in Two Worlds*, 107.

23. Kramer, *Lafayette in Two Worlds*, 105, 107.

24. *Genius of Liberty*, June 7, 1825, quoted in *A Pilgrimage of Liberty: A Contemporary Account of the Triumphal Tour of General Lafayette Through the Southern and Western States in 1825, as Reported by the Local Newspapers*, comp. and ed. Edgar Ewing Brandon (Athens, Ohio: Lawhead Press, 1944), 368-73.

25. Webster, "Bunker Hill Monument," 185. See also Webster, "The Greek Revolution" (speech delivered in the U.S. House of Representatives, January 19, 1824), in *Speeches of Daniel Webster*, ed. Tefft, 141-42, 157-58.

ette—the young French aristocrat who had left family, friends, and fortune to serve, at his own expense, in the American Revolution; and whose sole motivation was apparently a fervent desire to fight for the glorious cause of liberty. In a speech honoring Lafayette at a celebration in Milledgeville, Georgia, a city official rehearsed the story of Lafayette's service in the American Revolution, and then expressed "the hope that our country is destined to produce other Lafayettes, who profiting by your example and aided by the God of Battles, will give liberty and independence to nations now groaning under the yoke of tyranny and oppression."[26]

Lafayette's example apparently influenced at least three Americans to offer their services to the Greeks. One of them, Estwick Evans of New Hampshire, actually spent the month of July, 1825, in Greece.[27] Another volunteer was twenty-three-year-old Bedinger Morgan of Kentucky. He revealed his motivations in a long, semiliterate letter to Lafayette in which he requested the Marquis's aid and support for his venture, which he believed to be "congenial with your wishes and policy." Morgan explained that he had watched the struggle "for Grecian liberty" with considerable "interest and anxiety." It had partially succeeded. But the battle was not yet done. "The prayers of America has been put up for them," Morgan observed. "Our Congress has recognized them free and Independant." But "something else must be done[;] unless Individuals contribute there mite—Greece may yet be enslaved," he declared. "I therefore as an Individual of these United States—and a Sitizen of Kentucky—Volentarily step forward and tender to her my cirvaces my fortune and if necessary my life—with the full determination with her to live—or with her to perish—concurring in the sentiments contained in the American Declaration of Independance. . . . I feel it a duty to protect and assist so far as it is in my power the oppressed."[28]

26. Address of the intendant, Milledgeville, Georgia, March 27, 1825, quoted in Brandon, *Pilgrimage*, 135. See also, for a similar view, Nashville *Whig*, May 7, 14, 1825, quoted in Anne C. Loveland, *Emblem of Liberty: The Image of Lafayette in the American Mind* (Baton Rouge: Louisiana State University Press, 1971), 115. Henry Ware made an explicit call for volunteers in the Greek struggle at a meeting of the Phi Beta Kappa Society of Harvard College held in honor of Lafayette. Larrabee, *Hellas Observed*, 113.

27. Historian Stephen A. Larrabee speculates that Lafayette's tour "may have encouraged him to think of being something like his counterpart in Greece." Larrabee, *Hellas Observed*, 135-36, and see also 137, 316-17n.

28. Bedinger Morgan to "Friend of Washington," Russellvill Logan Ct [*sic*], Ky., May 20, 1825, in Arthur H. and Mary Marden Dean Lafayette Collection, Division of Rare and Manuscript Collections, Cornell University Library, Ithaca, New York, hereinafter cited as

Lloyd Kramer has told the story of a third American who volunteered his services to the Greeks. Samuel Gridley Howe was a young doctor from a prominent family in Boston. According to Kramer, he was not only influenced by the example of Lafayette, but also by the death of Byron and an unhappy love affair. Howe spent several years in Greece giving medical and humanitarian aid to the Greek people.[29]

Lafayette resumed his appeals to American political leaders for U.S. government intervention in the Greek revolution upon returning to France after his Triumphal Tour. In several letters he wrote in 1825-26 to Henry Clay, who had become Secretary of State, he consistently praised "Gallant Greece," citing the "admirable heroism" and "heroic resistance" of the people. They had been "abandoned . . . by all, and attacked or betrayed by many of the Christian powers." The United States remained their only hope. Reiterating his request for an American naval squadron, he declared that "every liberal man, or body of men" had a "moral obligation" to give the Greeks encouragement and assistance. These were arguments he had made before his tour. Now, in addition, he cited the "popular feeling" exhibited in America during that tour, as well as "the general feeling in Europe" in support of such aid. Another new argument appeared. Apparently the Greek revolution was not going well. In November 1825, Lafayette himself mentioned "the quarreling spirit of the Grecian chiefs, and abuses attending a long interruption of national Government." But in January 1826, he declared that "the bad situation of the Greeks has been exaggerated, even by well-meaning persons." He said such persons failed to appreciate the "elasticity" in the "revolutionary spirit of freedom." Lafayette repeatedly emphasized that *his* hopes for Greece had not been disappointed, that he remained optimistic about the result of the revolution.[30] But he knew from letters he received from his American friends that some of *them* had lost faith. For example, Richard Peters wrote to him in December 1826, "I never believed them [the Greeks] fit for a republican Government." He went on to complain that "the Greeks deceive our Judgments by our associating their ancient Fame

---

Dean Lafayette Collection.

29. Kramer, *Lafayette in Two Worlds*, 108-109. For more information on Howe, see Larrabee, *Hellas Observed*, 112-22, 166-75, and for accounts of other American participants in the Greek revolution, 95-112, 123-34, 144.

30. Lafayette to Clay, November 25, 1825, January 22, February 28, April 28, May 28, December 29, 1826, in *Life, Correspondence, and Speeches of Henry Clay*, IV: 132-33, 136, 137-38, 141-42, 154.

with their modern character. They are at least Semi barbarians; & it is to be regretted that so good a cause is in such incompetent hands."[31]

Perhaps such disillusionment was inevitable. Americans believed—or wanted to believe—that the European revolutions were inspired by their own exemplary revolution. Using the American Revolution as a standard, they expected the European revolutions to be moderate, relatively bloodless, and free of factionalism, and they protested any deviation from the model, ignoring the influence exerted by the different historical, political, social, and economic contexts in which the European revolutions occurred.

THE FRENCH REVOLUTION OF 1830

When news of the 1830 French Revolution reached the United States, there were celebrations in cities and towns across the nation, and private citizens wrote letters of congratulation to Lafayette expressing enthusiasm for the "glorious revolution."[32] The Marquis's acceptance of command of the National Guard was most encouraging. Josiah Quincy reported to Lafayette that some Americans had feared a repetition of the violent "convulsions" that had sabotaged the 1789 revolution. Thankfully, such anxiety proved "groundless," he observed. Indeed, Quincy pronounced the Revolution of 1830 a success; it had been "effected without other bloodshed, than that, which flowed in the first and inevitable combat!" In his view, the "virtue" and "moderation" of Lafayette's compatriots demonstrated that "the lapse and lessons of forty years had materially changed the character of the French people."[33]

31. Peters to Lafayette, December 1826, in Dean Lafayette Collection. See also Marshall to Lafayette, May 2, 1827, and Josiah Quincy to Lafayette, May 6, 1828, ibid.

32. Fish to Lafayette, September 22 and December 19, 1830, ibid. See also the following letters to Lafayette: E. Everett, October 29, 1830; A. H. Everett, September 15, 1830; E. Livingston, December 26, 1830; W. C. Rives, July 31, August 1, and November 8, 1830; John S. Cogdell, November 19, 1830; James G. King, October 1, 1830; Joseph S. Lewis, January 23, 1831, ibid.

33. Quincy to Lafayette, January 31, 1831, ibid. See also the following letters to Lafayette: E. Livingston, October 10, 1830; J. Brown, October 9, 1830; Philip Howe, September 28, 1830; Daniel Foster, November 22, 1830, ibid.; and James Monroe to a committee of Tammany Hall, 1831, in *The Writings of James Monroe, Including a Collection of His Public and Private Papers and Correspondence Now for the First Time Printed*, ed. Stanislaus Murray Hamilton (New York: G. P. Putnam's Sons, 1898-1903), VII: 220-21. For more qualified judgments of the Revolution of 1830, see John C. Calhoun to Lafayette, October

The notion that the French people had made considerable progress in acquiring a "respect for legality and good order" inspired confidence among Americans that under Lafayette's guidance, the French would this time be able to follow the American example, not only in revolting against oppression, but in establishing stable constitutional government.[34]

To be sure, France had instituted a constitutional monarchy, rather than a republican form of government, and Lafayette himself had approved that decision. Most of his American friends did not object. "For myself," James Madison wrote to Lafayette, "Republican as I am, I easily conceive that the Constitutional Monarchy adopted, may be as necessary to the actual condition of France, internal & external, as Mr. Jefferson thought the system, which left Louis XVI on the Throne, was an eligible accommodation to the then State of things."[35] Most of Lafayette's American correspondents thought that it was necessary to stop at constitutional monarchy not only to prevent a repetition of the anarchy and terror of the 1790s, but also to allow a period of time for the growth of knowledge and of experience in self-government. The moral transformation of the French people had not proceeded far enough to support a republican form of government.[36]

However, acceptance of constitutional monarchy did not mean giving up the American example of republican government. Madison favored a constitutional monarchy precisely because he believed it left open the opportunity to establish a republican government when "internal and external conditions" permitted. If and when such a change became possible, Madison urged Lafayette to consider "a federal system" similar to that of the United States.[37]

23, 1830, in Dean Lafayette Collection; and J. Q. Adams Diary, December 23, 1830, in *Memoirs of John Quincy Adams, Comprising Portions of His Diary from 1795 to 1848*, ed. Charles F. Adams (Philadelphia: J. B. Lippincott and Co., 1874-77), VII: 253.

34. See, for example, Albert Gallatin contrasting the revolutionaries of 1789 and 1830, in a November 1830, letter to Lafayette, quoted in Loveland, *Emblem of Liberty*, 120.

35. Madison to Lafayette, December 12, 1830, Dean Lafayette Collection. Jefferson's views of the Revolution of 1789 were published (before the Revolution of 1830) in the *Memoir, Correspondence, and Miscellanies, from the Papers of Thomas Jefferson*, ed. Thomas Jefferson Randolph (Charlottesville, VA: F. Carr, and Co., 1829), I: 56, 75-76, 81-82; IV: 246-48, 384.

36. See, for example, Gallatin's views on the "political education" of the French people, in a letter to Lafayette, November 1, 1830, quoted in Loveland, *Emblem of Liberty*, 121.

37. Madison to Lafayette, December 12, 1830, in Dean Lafayette Collection.

Some of Lafayette's American correspondents were less patient than Madison. They expected the French to follow the American example sooner rather than later. In 1831, Eliza P. Custis lectured Lafayette on what should have been done at the very beginning of the revolution. The peers and deputies should have dissolved themselves, she declared, and called a convention "to form a Constitution on liberal principles—have a Senate & deputies like ours or nearly so & give no King power to dissolve them nor to issue one ordanance [*sic*] of his own will." Of a Frenchman living in the United States, she told Lafayette, "His friends in france write him they wish the Americans would send some of their wise men to teach the french how to make good Laws—. . . ." She informed Lafayette how *she* would have responded to their request:

> I should have answer'd them . . . `you have the constitution of the United States—you have the constitutions of twenty four sovereign & independant States—have them translated, publish'd in your Paris newspapers, & circulated through all france—if after studying those constitutions & forms of government, which have made this Country the wonder of the world—the french will not rally Round the banner of freedom & . . . determine to secure a full representation & free constitution to their posterity neither could they be aroused to their duty, if all the Patriots of America went to instruct them—nor even if the Immortal Washington descended from heaven to tell them the blood of the Martyrs of July 1830 should not be shed in vain." And after all, the French did have Lafayette. America "speaks to you," Custis wrote, "& says . . . have a constitution—an elected senate—extend the right of voting, to all who possess one or two hundred francs—set the press free from all shackles—& allow your people to meet & debate as they wish--then may you say, the french are indeed free. . . .[38]

Custis expressed unqualified faith in the American example, but another American denied its validity for France in the 1830s. In a pamphlet addressed to Lafayette and published in August, 1831, an individual who called himself "A North American" criticized the Marquis for urging his countrymen "to follow the political examples we afford," while ignoring the one factor that differentiated the United States from France: "the great majority of people here, voters or not, are holders of land, in their own right, or, which is the same in the matter in question, may be so of many acres too, at their own discretion." Widespread land ownership gave American citizens "an

38. Eliza P. Custis to Lafayette, March 28, 1831, and July 23, 1831, ibid. See also Custis to Lafayette, September 6, 1830, and September 25, 1830, ibid.

interest . . . in the maintenance of law and order" that, in his view, landless people did not share. Lafayette had been urging the extension of the suffrage in France. The "North American" contended that enfranchising large numbers of unpropertied Frenchmen risked an upsurge of mob rule such as had reigned during the Revolution of 1789.[39]

Disappointment, even disillusionment, characterized the reaction of some Americans to the Revolution of 1830. Two years after its outbreak, Peter Jay proclaimed the futility, not just of the Revolution of 1830, but of all revolutions. He observed "a spirit of discontent" pervading Europe but declared it was "mingled with so much rancor and malevolence" that it inspired fear as well as hope. The present governments of Europe were "bad enough." Still, he asked, "is there reason to expect that the revolutionary Governments which may succeed them will be better?" As for France, its people were "not yet prepared for a republican Govt; such a one may be set up, but cannot last."[40]

Although many Americans were disappointed with the outcome of the French Revolution of 1830, most continued to regard Lafayette as "the staunch undeviating defender of . . . American principles."[41] They viewed his role in the Revolution of 1830 as a glorious consummation and vindication of his steadfast and selfless devotion to liberty. Even those who thought he had exercised bad judgment in putting Louis-Philippe on the throne believed he had acted disinterestedly and with good intentions. Untainted by the failure of the revolution, Lafayette remained until his death the trusted agent of the American mission.[42] Indeed, reverence for Lafayette continued

39. A North American, *To General Lafayette, United States, August 10, 1831* ([New York?], 1831]), 3, 5, 7, 9. The occasion for the pamphlet may have been Lafayette's manifesto to his constituents of Meaux defending the establishment of a "popular throne with republican institutions" and demanding, among other things, a widening of the suffrage. In support of such a measure Lafayette had cited "the illimitable suffrages of the United States." Lafayette offered the declaration of principles on beginning his campaign for re-election to the Chamber of Deputies following its dissolution on May 31. The letter was published in full in B. Sarrans, *Memoirs of General Lafayette and of the French Revolution of 1830* (London: Richard Bentley, 1832), II: 247-62.

40. Peter Jay to James Fenimore Cooper, February 21, 1832, in *Correspondence of James Fenimore Cooper*, ed. James Fenimore Cooper (New Haven: Yale University Press, 1922) I: 260-61.

41. Samuel F. B. Morse quoted in *Niles' Weekly Register*, September 1, 1832, p. 6.

42. See remarks of Americans quoted in Loveland, *Emblem of Liberty*, 129-30.

long after his death.[43] So did American support for the American mission. The history of the United States offers numerous examples of the American people debating when, where, how, and whether to pursue the American mission—in the late nineteenth and twentieth centuries, and even now in the twenty-first century.

43. See Loveland, *Emblem of Liberty*, chaps. 5 and 6.

5 Bridges to Freedom: Lafayette's Use of Revolutionary Rhetoric in the Political Strategies of his Tours

Robert Rhodes Crout

Historians and the general public have often used the term "Lafayette's tour" to refer to his 1824-25 visit to the United States. Yet Lafayette, the Frenchman who had come to America in 1777 as a Major General of the Continental Army, was the central figure in several other "tours." These included an earlier journey through ten American states shortly after the American Revolution in 1784 and a trip around central France in the summer of 1829. These three tours taken together reveal a pattern of Lafayette's development as a political figure as well as his expanding identity as "hero." The term "triumph" was often applied during this period to these travels to suggest an association between Lafayette and the neoclassical and republican tradition of "triumphal journeys," though such historic journeys admittedly had non-republican significance in the western tradition.[1] In the

1. The triumphal journey in the Western world has been the subject of several recent studies, whether covering ancient Rome, medieval Christendom, or the Early Modern era. Mary Beard has provided an important analysis of the archetype, the Roman triumphal parade. Her book has detailed the form and procedures that were painstakingly followed to qualify, then honor the hero. J. Doig in an important 1996 article in *Nottingham Medieval Studies* explains that northern European kingdoms also participated in similar royal events known as the "triumphal" progress or "joyous" entry, providing an opportunity for royal subjects to recognize and proclaim their monarch's authority and to welcome him upon his arrival in their city. Bonner Mitchell has pursued the subject with his study of Renaissance Italy. Mary Beard, *The Roman Triumph* (Cambridge: Harvard University Press, 2007); Victor E. Graham and W. McAllister Johnson, *The Paris Entries of Charles IX and Elizabeth of Austria, 1571* (Toronto: University of Toronto Press, 1975); Bonner Mitchell, *The Majesty of the State: Triumphal Progresses of Foreign Sovereigns in Renaissance Italy, 1494-1600* (Florence: Leo S. Olschki, 1986); J. Doig, "Propaganda and Truth: Henry V's Royal Progress in 1421," *Nottingham Medieval Studies* 40 (1996): 167-79. Earlier versions of portions of this paper were presented to the Southern Historical Association and

speeches and addresses Lafayette delivered in 1784, his republican and liberal vocabulary included such words and phrases as "brother," "union" or "federal union," "happiness," "commercial success" or "prosperity," "nation," "freedom" or "liberty," "rights of mankind," and "asylum." During the 1824-1825 tour, he used terms like "free," "republican," "usefulness," "improvement," "industry," "virtue," "enlightened," "toleration," "equal rights," "general philanthropy," "fraternity," "equality," and negative words such as "despotism" and "bigotry." In 1829 in France, he included expressions such as "*progressivement* [progressively]," "*liberté nationale* [national liberty]," "*volonté publique* [public will]," "*droits* [rights]," "*prosperité* [prosperity]," "*droits nationaux et sociaux* [national and social rights]," and negative words like "*usurpations* [usurpations]," "*l'arbitraire* [arbitrariness]," and "*oppression* [oppression]." His speeches, toasts, addresses, and gestures during these three tours were filled with the ideas and ideals of liberalism and republicanism.

Of these three tours, there has been no separate study of the first or the last, probably because popular and scholarly interest in the tour of 1824-25 has overshadowed the other two. Yet there are consistent patterns of speech from the three tours that are significant to understanding Lafayette and his development personally, politically, and as a historical figure. Lafayette's experiences in the American Revolution had taught him much about the practical political processes involved in creating a governmental system based on popular sovereignty that included individual freedoms and that promoted free trade balanced with a centralized foreign policy and a citizen military force. Along with his fellow officers in the Continental Army during the Revolution, Lafayette had experienced the problems of fractured American government and a weakened economy as well as the difficulties of rallying a civilian and citizen-soldier population against a world-power accused of "despotic" or "tyrannical" behavior. Scholars have documented elsewhere the experiences of Continental officers that led them to promote a stronger central authority.[2]

---

the Consortium on the Revolutionary Era 1750-1850. The author thanks the Consortium for permission to include portions from his paper that appeared in their *Selected Papers*. He also expresses appreciation to those who have contributed helpful suggestions: Stephen D. Carls, Edmund L. Drago, Stanley J. Idzerda, Jordan Kellman, Stuart Knee, and Neal Polhemus.

2. For example, as William Benton has stated, "Revolutionary officers . . . were among the advocates of a stronger central government through the Constitution," Pennsylvania Revolutionary Officers and the Federal Constitution," *Pennsylvania History* 31 [1964], 419. Sidney Kaplan was more specific in stating that it was Continental offi-

When Lafayette returned in 1824-25, he saw much progress from that immense post-revolutionary era, and he claimed that progress as the tangible legacy of those revolutionary principles. Yet he also observed tensions in American society, and he gently but firmly and repeatedly encouraged Americans to become engaged in resolving the internal problems and aiding republican causes elsewhere.

Back in France in the years before the Revolution of 1830, Lafayette applied many of the principles he had supported in the American Revolution and the 1789 French Revolution (and ideas even more radical than those) in urging political reform in his native France. He also used the political techniques he had refined on the earlier two tours in America to promote his liberal (and republican) agenda in a tour throughout central France during the summer before the Revolution of 1830. As he told Americans in 1784 and in 1824-25 and the French in 1829, the model that Americans used would have global implications.

These three tours reflected the rapidly developing values of new political techniques and a new era that was developing in the transatlantic world. They were of course about issues such as popular sovereignty, individual rights and liberties, and a greater sense of inclusiveness. They were also about political techniques, such as the public assembly, the directed appeal to a specific constituency, and the banquet discourse that included both speeches and toasts. Yet Lafayette was not merely concerned about the spoken words themselves; he was also interested in developing the means to distribute them to a wider reading public. The journalistic practice of the period was to lift articles from a distant newspaper, reprint them locally (usually with an acknowledgment of the source), and thereby pass the news on to a wider audience. Until the development of the telegraph in the 1840s-1860s, this was the manner in which most news spread in the eighteenth- and early nineteenth-century Atlantic world. To publicize his words, Lafayette mastered the practice of what today we would call the "press release." He mailed newspapers to friends across the Atlantic. Often he or his son serving as transcriber of his speeches and toasts would submit copies of the speeches directly to journalists or journalists' friends for publication. Lafayette was

---

cers. "Veteran Officers and Politics in Massachusetts, 1783-1787," *William and Mary Quarterly*, 3rd series, 9 (1952): 29-57. For the experiences of the war itself, see Merrill Jensen, "The Idea of a National Government during the American Revolution," *Political Science Quarterly* 58 (1943): 356-79, and E. James Ferguson, "The Nationalists of 1781-1783 and the Economic Interpretation of the Constitution," *Journal of American History* 56 (1969):241-61.

thus actively involved not merely in speaking but in spreading those words and ideas.[3] Though these tours began simply as ceremonial celebrations of past victories, Lafayette's understanding of their potential expanded over time to transform them into political actions to promote a far more important and complex agenda for the future—both the acknowledgment of past accomplishments and a statement of unfinished political business.

* * *

Lafayette's 1784 tour had begun innocently as an opportunity to celebrate the Revolutionary victory with and among his American friends at his earliest convenient opportunity. However, shortly after arriving, the tour took on a very different meaning as he observed the young country at a critical juncture. When Lafayette had left America in December 1781 after the Yorktown campaign, he intended to return soon thereafter for the remainder of the war.[4] Back in France in 1782 he continued to function as an intermediary between the Americans and the French and assisted the diplomats. He briefly served in a French military capacity at Cadiz with D'Estaing to prepare for a final allied "big push" that never came about. Lafayette was not in America for the celebrations at the close of the war, and he had to console himself with seemingly endless congratulatory letters to his friends and comrades.

From the time of his arrival in France, he had written his American

3. Transcriptions and drafts of Lafayette's speeches and addresses not only survive in the collections of his papers at Chateau de LaGrange, Cornell University, and the Archives Nationales of France, they are also scattered in repositories around the places he visited, obviously having been prepared for inclusion in local newspapers. Copies in the handwritings of Lafayette, his son, and his secretary Levasseur may be found at the Massachusetts Historical Society, the Library of Virginia, the Historical Society of Pennsylvania, Lafayette College, the North Carolina Department of Archives and History, the Maine Historical Society, the Vermont Historical Society, the Morristown National Historical Park, and the Henry E. Huntington Library and Art Gallery.

4. Though there is no separate interpretive study of the 1784 tour, see volume five of Stanley J. Idzerda and Robert Rhodes Crout, eds., *Lafayette in the Age of the American Revolution: Selected Letters and Papers, 1776-1790*, 5 vols. to date (Ithaca, New York: Cornell University Press, 1977-) (hereafter cited as *Lafayette Papers*). For the classic account of the 1784 tour, see Louis Gottschalk, *Lafayette between the American and the French Revolution 1783-1789* (Chicago: University of Chicago Press, 1950), esp. 83-150. See Lafayette to Nathanael Greene, November 22, 1781, in *Lafayette Papers*, 4:438-39.

friends about his plans to return. They had responded to those letters with reports of their own efforts for the future, a future of both political and economic American independence. Soon Lafayette began to realize that he had another mission: to build closer relations between France and the new nation. He prepared extensive observations on American trade for the French royal council. He also served his American merchant friends as their informal agent and promoter in France. Yet he was still anxious to return to America.[5]

Lafayette planned to arrive in America in May 1784, a proposal this time delayed by his efforts in France to gain more commercial concessions from the French government for the Americans. To his close friend George Washington he spoke only about his cherished personal memories and fraternal bonds of affection, anticipating the upcoming general meeting of the Society of Cincinnati:

> When I think this letter will be read among representatives from all the lines of the army, my heart is glowing with all the unbounded sentiments of affection and gratitude. . . . Never can my heart forget the return of affection I have particularly obtained, the numberless obligations I am under to my dear brother officers, and the happy hours, the happiest in my life, which I have past in their company . . . [I] am panting for the instant when I may be blessed with a sight of the American shore.

In another, more personal letter to Washington that same day, he added, "You will see a vessel coming up the Potomac, and out of that vessel will your friend jump with a panting heart and all the feelings of perfect happiness." By April 1784 with his projects successfully completed, Lafayette suggested in a letter to Jeremiah Wadsworth that he might arrive in America by June. Lafayette explained to a skeptical John Adams that he was not motivated as he had been earlier by the revolution or the war-making. "Now I am going for the people, and my motives are that I love them and they love me. . . .[6]

5. For an example of Lafayette's intention to return soon to America, see Lafayette to John Adams, March 27, 1782, "I will remain some weeks more in France" (*Lafayette Papers*, 5:19). As the treaty developed, Lafayette thought he would carry it back to America (ibid., 69); "Observations on Commerce between France and the United States," [December 13, 1783] (ibid., 168-75).

6. Lafayette to Washington, two letters of March 9, 1784; Lafayette to Wadsworth, April 19, April 22, 1784; Lafayette to Adams, April 9, 1784 (ibid., 207, 209, 214).

When he arrived in New Jersey in early August, Lafayette proclaimed to Samuel Adams his pleasure at seeing an America free of war. In Philadelphia, he conveyed his regards to his "dear brother officers" of the Pennsylvania Line when they thanked him for his "noble example." Yet before he left Philadelphia, he began to perceive a crisis on the horizon. Of those who rode out to welcome Lafayette to Philadelphia on August 9 was the Superintendant of Finances Robert Morris. Lafayette met again to talk with Morris on August 11 and 12 about what Morris described in his diary as "the Situation of American Affairs." What Morris meant is unclear, but Morris was writing at the time to his other correspondents about the payment of the interest on French loans to the Americans and the settlement of state advances on continental accounts.[7] It is clear that Lafayette began to perceive a new role for his American travels, that of a beneficent but distant friend and adviser, one knowledgeable of the American condition but not involved domestically in the issues of a stronger union, promoter of more effective economic and military establishments. As he wrote to his wife Adrienne, "In my present situation I like to think that my influence may not be useless to the domestic interests of the United States, to the union that should exist between them, in short, to the federal union."

An event occurred six days after writing to his wife that definitively ended Lafayette's original plan for a simple celebratory tour, an event in Philadelphia that confirmed his concerns over the fragility of the American confederation. The Articles of Confederation had required that one delegate from each state in the Continental Congress remain in Philadelphia for the Committee of States to continue functioning as the central government. On August 19 attendance fell below the necessary quorum. That event struck Lafayette particularly hard and confirmed whatever concerns his conversations with Morris had raised. He lost no time in complaining to the remaining members of Congress about the impression this adjournment would make abroad. One delegate reported him as saying, "No step since the peace will more deeply wound our interests in the courts of Europe."[8]

7. E. James Ferguson, et al., eds., *Papers of Robert Morris*, 9 vols. (Pittsburgh: University of Pittsburgh Press, 1973-1999, hereafter *Morris Papers*), 9: 474-485. Note that Ferguson claimed Morris as a central figure in the emerging nationalist movement (Ferguson, 'The Nationalist Movement," 244).

8. Lafayette to Samuel Adams, August 7, ibid., 233; Lafayette to Committee of Officers of the Late Pennsylvania Line, August 9, ibid., 234; Lafayette to Adrienne, 13 August, ibid., 235; Jacob Read to Benjamin Guerard, September 9, Paul H. Smith and others, eds., *Letters of Delegates to Congress* 26 vols. (Washington: Library of Congress, 1976-

After a brief visit to Mount Vernon to see Washington, Lafayette moved on to Baltimore. There in early September he reminded his audience of the new commercial possibilities that awaited their merchants with four free ports in France for American goods (for which he had earlier lobbied).[9] From there he continued on to New York City and traveled up to Albany, finally reaching Fort Schuyler to assist the Americans in their negotiations with the Iroquois chiefs. As warrior and subject of the king of France and having been adopted by them in 1778 and given the name "Kayewla," Lafayette spoke as "an sachem of the family," a role he could assume effectively. Lafayette's appeals to the Iroquois chiefs had the desired effect, and the American effort to negotiate a successful treaty with them proved successful.[10]

Financier Robert Morris writing to the president of Congress proclaimed his admiration of the young Frenchman: "The unexampled attention to every American interest which this gentleman has exhibited cannot fail to excite the strongest emotion in his favor. . . ."[11] Lafayette then began to realize that his words might have even greater weight among his American friends than he had anticipated. As Jefferson was preparing to leave to become U.S. minister to France, Lafayette wrote him that he intended to go to the meeting of the Continental Congress at Trenton and pay his "respects." He added, "God grant such a federative system may be fairly followed by all the states as will insure their eternal union and of course their interior happiness, commercial wealth, and national consequence!" This remark revealed

2000), 21: 789. On the role of Continental officers in the politics of the Confederation period, see note 3, above.

9. Lafayette to Citizens of Baltimore, September 1 (*Lafayette Papers*, 5: 241). The address was reprinted in the *New-York Packet* on September 9 and in the [Philadelphia] *Pennsylvania Mercury* on September 10.

10. Lafayette to Adrienne, October 4 (*Lafayette Papers*, 5: 260). On Lafayette's earlier adoption by the Iroquois, see *Lafayette Papers*, 1: 247. Lafayette wrote to Alexander Hamilton on October 8, "It has been found that my influence with the Indians, both friendly and hostile tribes, was much greater than the commissioners and even myself had conceived." Ibid., 263-64. See another version of the same comment in his letter to Washington of the same date, ibid., 264. One of the commissioners, James Madison, agreed with Lafayette's assessment of his role; see Madison to Jefferson, October, 17, William T. Hutchinson, et al., eds., *The Papers of James Madison, Congressional Series*, 17 vols. (Chicago: University of Chicago Press, and Charlottesville: University Press of Virginia, 1962-1991), 8: 118-21.

11. Robert Morris to President of Congress, September 30 (*Morris Papers*, 9: 537).

the new direction that Lafayette found his tour taking. The tour was no longer simply a visit to old friends, but had now become an opportunity for Lafayette to encourage and promote the adoption of a stronger American union. At the same time Lafayette realized he was a French subject and as such was constantly concerned that his speeches might be taken as remarks authorized by the French government. Whenever this occurred in print, he promptly contacted the American newspapers requesting appropriate corrections.[12]

While he gave a series of fraternal speeches to groups such as the veterans of the Massachusetts and the Rhode Island lines, to the Rhode Island governor and general assembly, he more seriously urged, "May these rising states unite in every measure as they have united in their struggles; and may their wealth and consequence . . . baffle the calculations of jealousy and fulfill the enthusiastic hopes of patriotism." Similarly he wished to the Maryland general assembly that "this state . . . will . . . in the federal union so necessary to all, attain the highest degree of particular happiness and prosperity." To longtime friends such as David Humphreys, Washington's former aide-de-camp, Lafayette suggested that the approaching winter would be "an important crisis for the interior arrangements of America so far at least as respects federal union, commercial system, and militia establishment."[13]

Lafayette dealt with the approaching crisis most comprehensively in his important public address before the Continental Congress at its meeting in Trenton on December 11:

12. Lafayette to Vergennes, October 12, *Lafayette Papers,* 5: 270. Unfortunately none of Lafayette's letters to these American newspapers appears to have survived. Lafayette's early relationship with newspaper editors would be a pattern throughout his lifetime as he was very sensitive to and aware of the growing importance of public opinion in the Atlantic world.

13. Lafayette to the Massachusetts Line, October 16 (Boston) *American Herald,* October 18; the original corrected draft of his remarks is in the Maine Historical Society: S. H. Fogg Autograph Collection); Lafayette to the Rhode Island Line, October 25 (Boston) *Massachusetts Centinel,* October 30; Lafayette to Rhode Island Assembly, October 26 (Providence) *United States Chronicle,* November 3; Lafayette to General Assembly of Maryland, November 30 (Annapolis) *Maryland Gazette,* December 9; Lafayette to Humphreys, October 31, *Lafayette Papers,* 5: 277. On Lafayette's use of "brotherhood" and masculinity themes, see my "Brotherhood and Fraternité in the Transatlantic: Codes of Masculinity in the American Continental Army, the French National Guard, and Lafayette," *Selected Papers from the 2009 Consortium on the Revolutionary Era, 1750-1850* (forthcoming).

> I am happy to observe the prevailing disposition of the people to strengthen the confederation, preserve public faith [meaning credit], regulate trade, and in a proper guard over continental magazines and frontier posts, in a general system of militia, in foreseeing attention to the navy, to insure every kind of safety, [then added his most famous phrase] May this immense temple of freedom ever stand as a lesson to oppressors, an example to the oppressed, a sanctuary for the rights of Mankind![14]

Back in France, Lafayette actively and regularly wrote to his American friends to encourage a stronger central government and to support American commercial ventures in France. To Nathanael Greene, he responded to an inquiry about what effect stronger Congressional control over trade and public credit might have in France. Lafayette's reply? "The effect . . . would be greater than can be imagined." He urged that Americans lose no time. That same day he wrote to Richard Henry Lee, "Above all . . . do attend to the confederation, to union, and harmony, and every regulation that can give security to commerce, energy to the government, faith to the public creditors." Furthermore he warned Connecticut merchant Jeremiah Wadsworth that no American goods were arriving in France and that such inaction might lead the French government to suspend their regular packets between the two countries.[15] For much of the next few years Lafayette spent a great deal of time urging the Americans to stronger central government and supporting what would soon become the new American federal constitution.

What then can we conclude from Lafayette's 1784 tour? It began quite simply and literally as a reunion tour, an opportunity for Lafayette to see old friends and to be honored for his participation in the American Revolution. Yet after arriving in America, Lafayette soon came to realize that winning independence from Britain was not the end of the American Revolution. To succeed as an independent nation would require a stronger political union and a central government that could exercise power over the states, especial-

14. Lafayette, Address to Congress, December 11, *Lafayette Papers*, 5: 281. The text appeared in the *Pennsylvania Packet* on December 18. That same day Lafayette gave an important speech to the New Jersey legislature, wishing "the blessings of this revolution, so nobly purchased, will be eternally secured in the united strength and wisdom of the federal republic" (Burlington) *New-Jersey Gazette*, December 27, also appearing in the *Maryland Gazette*, January 6 1785).

15. Lafayette to Greene, March 16, 1785, *Lafayette Papers*, 5: 305; Lafayette to Lee, March 16, ibid., 308; Lafayette to Wadsworth, April 16, ibid., 318.

ly in areas of commerce, credit, and foreign policy. By the middle of his tour Lafayette began to speak publicly in support of this agenda. After his return to France in 1785 Lafayette undertook a spirited letter writing campaign for an empowered federal system.

* * *

The 1784 tour served as a template for Lafayette, one whose techniques he used astutely during his 1824-25 tour of America. Though the later tour also involved many social and ceremonial events, it also included politically charged speeches and appearances for which Lafayette had a complex, specific, and conscious agenda. That agenda included both foreign and domestic issues, using his status as an authentic hero of the American Revolution to remind Americans of the unfinished vision of the founders.[16]

The U. S. agenda included rallying private and public support for overseas republican causes in Latin America, Spain, Greece, and Italy. The American domestic agenda included support for programs and legislation to resolve problems such as slavery through colonization efforts in Liberia and Haiti and emancipation experiments such as Nashoba. Lafayette also supported the expansion of public works that would develop the American economy and tie the states closer together, such as canals and highways, agricultural experimentation, and technological innovation.

In addition to his support of a distinctly American agenda, Lafayette also promoted liberal and republican causes in Europe by publicizing the accomplishments of America's republican virtue through the distribution of reports about his tour in European liberal papers. He accomplished this by

16. Anne C. Loveland's book, the first study to draw heavily from the rich Cornell University collection of Lafayette manuscript materials, remains the standard interpretation of the 1824-25 tour, *Emblem of Liberty: The Image of Lafayette in the American Mind* (Baton Rouge: Louisiana State University Press, 1971). Her later thoughts appear in her essay, "Lafayette's Farewell Tour," pp. 63-90 in Stanley J. Idzerda, et al., eds., *Lafayette Hero of Two Worlds: The Art and Pageantry of His Farewell Tour of America, 1824-1825* (New York, NY: The Queens Museum, 1989). Another important view is that of Fred Somkin, *Unquiet Eagle: Memory and Desire in the Idea of American Freedom, 1815-1860* (Ithaca, NY: Cornell University Press, 1967). An excellent analysis of its significance is Sylvia Neely, "The Politics of Liberty in the Old World and the New: Lafayette's Return to America in 1824," *Journal of the Early Republic* 6 (1986): 151-71. Alan R. Hoffman has provided a much improved and updated translation of the 1829 account of the trip by Lafayette's secretary Auguste Levasseur, *Lafayette in America in 1824 and 1825* (Manchester, New Hampshire: Lafayette Press, Inc., 2006).

forwarding speeches, addresses, and news articles from the American newspapers to his friends in France for inclusion in French newspapers. Liberal British newspapers and magazines also served as other sources of information as they were forwarded across the channel to France. So Lafayette's tour of 1824-25 served not only to promote his American agenda but also to support his European one.[17]

Following the death of his wife in 1807 Lafayette had hoped to visit America during the Napoleonic Wars, but his plans continued to be delayed because there was a general concern that Lafayette might not be able to secure a vessel for the return to France for some time. As the restoration of the French monarchy brought a more active role for Lafayette in French politics, he again hesitated. Lafayette wrote Revolutionary War veteran Joseph Wheaton in December 1823 that as soon as he could do it "with a safe conscience, I shall indulge my ardent wish to visit the happy shores of the United States."[18] Lafayette began to solicit through his correspondence a formal American invitation, and his defeat in the Chamber of Deputies election in the spring of 1824 only confirmed the plan. Family deaths and his own illness further delayed him. The formal invitation from President Mon-

17. Robert Rhodes Crout, "Lafayette's Tour," in *Encyclopedia of the Early Republic and Antebellum America*, ed. Christopher Bates (Armonk, New York: M.E. Sharpe, Inc., 2010). See especially Sylvia Neely's article cited in footnote one. George Armstrong has considered the 1824-25 tour as an example of American "civil religion" in his *Politics and Religious Consciousness in America* (New Brunswick: Transaction Books, 1984), 210-15. The French monarchy's reaction to Lafayette's visit is made clear through an anonymous September 9 letter from Paris published in the Washington *National Intelligencer* on October 22: "We had announced in our paper of today the arrival of General Lafayette at New York. . . . The censorship struck out this article, excepting three lines. . . ." Another anonymous letter of September 10 from Paris suggested, "Should you send any newspapers or publications relative to our friend the General, direct to Mr.—, with request to send by private hand or diligence; don't put my name or Paris on the superscription. . . . By and by, when we get matter enough, the whole of your doings will be given in a pamphlet" (Ibid., October 25, 1824).

18. Lafayette had written to Jefferson on September 20, 1810, "I have very *eagerly* [my emphasis] thought of going over with General Armstrong . . . had it not been the unanimous opinion of people knowing . . . that no precaution or assurance could secure a return" (Jefferson Papers, Library of Congress, Washington D.C.). Gilbert Chinard transcribes the word as "largely" in his *Letters of Lafayette and Jefferson* (Baltimore; Johns Hopkins University Press, 1929), 318. Lafayette to Joseph Wheaton, December 20, 1823, *National Intelligencer*, February 28, 1824. The text was reprinted in many American newspapers.

roe and the Congress offered an official cover to the widely known secret of Lafayette's desire for the journey. Lafayette would take the opportunities of his appearances, his speeches, addresses, and toasts to further his agendas.[19]

The first American city Lafayette visited in 1824 was New York. Its complex constituencies (so reflective of American society at the end of the Era of Good Feelings) provided him with a pattern of social groups to address and a pattern of issues and words with which to address them. His remarks in New York City provide a paradigm of the vocabulary in his speeches and addresses as he moved the next thirteen months through every state of the American union.

Upon landing in New York City harbor on August 15, 1824, Lafayette found himself the subject of the wild republican adulation of the young nation as it approached the fiftieth anniversary of the Battle of Bunker Hill. In the harbor he immediately fulfilled one of the purposes of his voyage as he greeted his old friends and fellow soldiers Marinus Willett, Philip Van Cortland, Matthew Clarkson, Richard Varick, and Nathaniel Platt. Lafayette engaged in extensive conversation with Willett as the two recounted their activities in the Revolution. The pattern was repeated with other veterans all over the United States. All were astounded at Lafayette's ability to recall minor details and names from the Revolution in his travels across America.[20]

References to the classical Roman triumph took over as the Frenchman reached Manhattan Island—a triumphal parade, temporary arches raised and painted to resemble those of ancient Rome with watchwords of the Revolution included, and speeches that praised both deeds and virtues. For each

19. On January 8 an October 26 letter from Lafayette to John Brannan stated, "A visit to the United States, which I may be allowed to take, once more going home, would be to me a source of inexpressible delight" (*National Intelligencer*, January 8). Members of Congress who were aware of Lafayette's widely broadcast desire for the visit included: Louisiana Congressman John Brent who had seen a letter from Lafayette to Mr. Davezac of New Orleans (not found); Edward Livingston of Louisiana had received a similar letter (not found); Congressman Mitchell produced a letter to Mr. [Marinus] Willett of New York (not found); Virginian Andrew Stevenson produced a letter of November 25 to a "distinguished citizen" [perhaps Lafayette's letter of that date to Monroe in which he wrote, "I more and more look forward to the day when, with a safe conscience, it shall be my happy lot to find myself on American ground" (NIC: Lafayette Collection, box 25, folder 38); debate on January 13, *National Intelligencer*, 14 January 1825]. On Lafayette's delay, see Lafayette to John Dyson, August 6, 1824 (Manuscript Collection, Morristown National Historical Park, Morristown, New Jersey).

20. (New York City) *Advocate*, August 17, 1825.

of the different constituencies (municipal authorities, scholarly societies, academic bodies, professional assemblies, French descendants, revolutionary veterans including Societies of Cincinnati, Masonic assemblies, and representatives of special groups) Lafayette developed particular vocabularies.

When New York Mayor William Paulding reported to him, "The people of the United States look up to you as to one of their most honored parents —the country cherishes you as one of the most beloved of her sons."[21] Lafayette replied in part:

> . . . the recollection of the many respected friends and dear companions no more to be found on this land, the pleasure to recognize those who have survived, this immense concourse of a free republican population who so kindly welcome me, . . . have excited sentiments to which no human language can be adequate.[22]

To the New-York Historical Society, the first among many scholarly societies he would address, Lafayette proclaimed, ". . . notwithstanding the combinations made elsewhere by despotism and aristocracy against those sacred rights of mankind, immense majorities in other countries shall not in vain observe the happiness and prosperity of a free, virtuous, and enlightened people."[23]

To the president, trustees, and faculty of New York's Columbia College, Lafayette offered his sympathies for the college's losses during the revolution but his joy "in the happy change that had taken place—and in the present visible prosperity of the institution" and in his hopes for "the increasing usefulness and reputation of Columbia College."[24] When the New York City Bar recalled to Lafayette's memory Hamilton, Lafayette replied in speaking of the Constitution, ". . . to anyone, who with an American heart has had the opportunities of a comparison with other countries, the blessings of those

21. *Mercantile Advertiser* (New York City), August 18, 1825. The draft manuscript is in Miscellaneous Manuscripts, Paulding, New-York Historical Society, New York City, New York

22. Lafayette's autograph response is found in the Archives de LaGrange-Bléneau, Courpalay, France (hereafter ALG), cote 270, no. 1.

23. Lafayette had originally written in his draft a much more hostile "in spite of" instead of "notwithstanding" (ALG: cote 270, no. 2).

24. A summary of Lafayette's remarks appears in Edgar Ewing Brandon, *Lafayette Guest of the Nation* (Oxford, Ohio: The Oxford Historical Press, 1950), 1: 190.

institutions must appear still more conspicuous."[25]

Though Lafayette did not present a special address to his beloved fellow veterans and their descendants in the New York chapter of the Society of the Cincinnati when he met with them, he did offer them a toast that would encapsulate his thoughts. "The sacred principles for which we fought and bled—liberty, equality, national independence—may every nation of the earth in adopting them drink a bumper to the old Continental Army."[26] To the first assembly of native Frenchmen and persons of French ancestry he would address, Lafayette declared, "Do not let us despair, Gentlemen, of the cause of liberty; it is still dear to the hearts of Frenchmen, and we shall one day have the felicity of seeing it established in our beloved country."[27]

Lafayette held his first meeting with Masonic groups in New York City on September 11, 1824, though his remarks do not appear to have been recorded. His remarks to the Masons at Troy, New York, were summarized in the local press as an acknowledgment that he had "always respected the institution" and was gratified by this interview with his "brethren." As he traveled around America, his words warmed at other Masonic events around the United States and eventually appeared in print if only in occasional summary, perhaps a concession to the secrecy of the proceedings.[28]

These several New York City speeches to specific groups set a tone for Lafayette throughout the tour. They established a pattern of speech-making and a particular vocabulary that unfolded throughout the next thirteen months. For example, the remarks he delivered to the New York City mayor expressed Lafayette's reaction to the development of American urban centers during the preceding fifty years, such as their constitutional principles, technological achievements, their increasing sophistication, and growth deep into the wildernesses. Lafayette spoke in similar terms before the civic authorities in Portsmouth, New Hampshire; Sterling and Worcester, Massachusetts; Albany and Troy, New York; about the economic and social progress these cities had made, emphasizing words like "improvement" and

25. The text of this speech is in ibid., 1: 47. Lafayette had originally written "forcibly felt" instead of "conspicuous" (ALG: cote 270, no. 3).

26. Ibid., 1: 186.

27. Ibid. The French text of Lafayette's remarks has not been located.

28. The remarks to Lafayette and his reply at the September 11 first Masonic meeting with New York's "Knights Templar" have not survived, nor his reply during his visit with the Royal Arch Masons in Troy (Brandon, *Lafayette Guest of the Nation*, 1: 199, 249).

"prosperity." "Those wildernesses rank among the most populous and best cultivated parts of the Union," he said. To the arrangements committee at Frederick, Maryland, he expressed his gratification to see their happy valley "where Agricultural and manufacturing industry practiced by a rapidly increasing population are the reward of your patriotic and domestic virtues. . . ." To the intendant (mayor) of Charleston, South Carolina, Lafayette remarked on the changes he observed there. "I find it in possession of the independence, republican institutions and prosperity for which we have fought. . . ." To the arrangements committee at Cincinnati, he noted "the wonders of creation and improvement which have happily raised this part of the Union to its present high degree of importance, prosperity and happiness." To the mayor of Buffalo, he complimented the village on "its wonderful improvements. . . ."[29]

As with his address to the New York Historical Society, Lafayette's speeches to other scholarly and scientific societies repeated his expressions about a "free, virtuous, and enlightened people." Though his exact remarks to the American Philosophical Society in Philadelphia appear not to have survived, their summary indicates that he "declared the high sense he had ever entertained of the honor of being one of the members."[30] To the Maryland Agricultural Society, Lafayette expressed "a deep interest in whatever may contribute to improvements in agriculture. . . ." To a student debating organization of budding scholars (known as the Enosinian Society) at the District of Columbia's Columbian College (now George Washington University), Lafayette was more particular: "Such a spirit in the Sons of Liberty is well calculated to preserve and recommend that happy system of free government, the operation of which, combining knowledge with patriotism, renders the U. States great and prosperous."[31]

29. Brandon, *Lafayette Guest of the Nation*, 1: 149, 162, 240, 247; Edgar Ewing Brandon, ed., A *Pilgrimage of Liberty: A Contemporary Account of the Triumphal Tour of General Lafayette . . . as Reported by the Local Newspapers* (Athens, Ohio: The Lawhead Press, 1944) 67, 323, 399. Lafayette's remarks at "Frederick Town" are found in ALG, cote 270A, no. 38.

30. The account from the Philadelphia *National Gazette* is quoted in J. Bennett Nolan, "Lafayette and the American Philosophical Society," *Proceedings of the American Philosophical Society* 73 (1934): 125.

31. Brandon, *Lafayette Guest of the Nation*, 3: 186; *American Farmer*, October 15, 1824. On Lafayette and the Maryland Agricultural Society, see Lucretia Ramsey Bishko, "Lafayette and the Maryland Agricultural Society, 1824-1832," *Maryland Historical Society* 70 (1975): 45-67.

Lafayette also spoke to groups that reflected his interests in the new society though perhaps were not yet part of the American power elite. Before audiences at female academies such as the Troy New York Female Seminary, the "female department" of the Free School Society of New York City, and the Female Academy in Lexington, Kentucky, Lafayette returned their expressions of regard and reminded them of his daughters and granddaughters, who had (unknown to these audiences) been brought up at his LaGrange residence and his Paris soirées to participate equally with men in the philosophical and political discussions of the time.[32]

Among the most important groups Lafayette regularly spoke to during his tour were Masonic assemblies, though the texts usually did not appear in print. To the Grand Lodge of Delaware, he appealed:

> Freemasonry was distinguished for the enlightened liberality of its principles. It inculcated unlimited toleration of religious opinions; and although as a society masons did not interfere with politics, they considered every member as a brother and as standing upon the same natural level; Freemasonry in these respects favors liberty and equality, the foes of tyrants...

In his remarks to the Masonic lodge in Augusta, Georgia, he expressed his attachment to "their institutions, thinking that such solemn engagements to equality and philanthropy could not but be useful to the cause of freedom, whether the Brethren reflected on themselves or were in communication with other parts of mankind. . . ."[33] To the New York City Bar, Lafayette spoke of the advantages of a republican government and legal system. To the bar of Philadelphia, he reminded them of the lawyers who had served the American cause and "the cause of mankind" during the Revolution. To the lawyers of Harrisburg, Pennsylvania, he recalled, "In all countries,

32. Brandon, *Lafayette Guest of the Nation*, 1: 195-96, 249-50, Brandon, *A Pilgrimage of Liberty*, 301-304. On Lafayette's relations with his granddaughters and his views on women, see my "Lafayette's Developing Liberal Agenda and its Implications for Proto-Feminism," *The 2003 Consortium on the Revolutionary Era: Selected Papers*, (forthcoming).

33. Brandon, *Lafayette Guest of the Nation*, 2: 113; Brandon, *A Pilgrimage of Liberty*, 128. A copy of Lafayette's remarks in Augusta in the handwriting of his son appears to indicate the practice of distributing copies of Lafayette's remarks to the local newspapers was a responsibility of his son or his secretary. Usually, once printers set such copies in type, they discarded the originals. This manuscript copy survives in the John Shaw Billings Scrapbooks, no. 45, Caroliniana Library, University of South Carolina, Columbia, South Carolina.

sir, where the rights of mankind have been defended, your profession has proved and still now is eminently distinguished for the number and talents of the supporters it has given to the cause of freedom . . ."[34]

Finally, Lafayette's remarks to the French in New York City were repeated in similar form to French communities in Philadelphia, Baltimore, Charleston, and Savannah. He compared the successes of the American Revolution with the benefits of the French Revolution momentarily delayed by the Restoration monarchy and made pointed references to earlier despotisms. In Philadelphia he recalled 1789: "You are right to think that this first impetus of '89 has despite our misfortunes greatly improved the situation of the French people; I share your wishes and your hope for the freedom of our country . . ." In Baltimore, he joined "in your good wishes for the universal liberty of our native country. . ."[35] In Charleston he added, "When about fifty years ago I landed on these shores . . . I had the gratification to find amongst the most distinguished patriots of South-Carolina, many descendants from those Frenchmen the victims of the despotism and bigotry of other times." [36] In Savannah, he responded, "I see myself thus welcomed by those of my French fellow countrymen and French descendants who on this happy American land found an asylum against very different persecutions but all rejected by the true spirit of liberty. . . ."[37]

For American academicians, Lafayette had a message even more direct than the one he had given at Columbia College in New York City. To the

34. The address to the Philadelphia bar is in ALG, cote 270, no. 17 ter. That to the lawyers of Harrisburg is in Ibid., no. 51.

35. ". . . Vous avés raison de penser que cette premiere impulsion de 89 a malgré nos malheurs grandement amelioré la situation du people francais; je partage vos voeux et votre espoir pour la liberté de notre patrie. . . ." (ALG, cote 270, no. 19). The French text of his Baltimore remarks has not been found (Brandon, *Lafayette Guest of the Nation*, 2: 132).

36. Brandon, *Pilgrimage of Liberty*, 80-81. Brandon omitted the original French, but it appeared in a local newspaper: "Lorsque j'arrivai il y a près de cinquante ans . . . j'eus le plaisir de trouver parmi les patriotes les plus distingués de la Caroline, beaucoup de descendans de ces Français qui furent les victimes du despotisme et de la bigoterie d'un autretems. . . ." (*Charleston Courier*, March 18, 1825)

37. "Je me vois aussi accueilli par celles de mes compatriotes Francais et descendans de Francais, qui sur cette heureuse terre Américaine ont trouvé un asyle contre des persecutions bien diverses mais toutes réprouvées par le véritable esprit de Liberté . . ." (*An Account of the Reception of General Lafayette in Savannah* [Savannah, 1825], 37-38).

president of Brunswick College in Portland, he extended his greetings to a college "where young republicans, the hope of the country, are instructed in every literary and scientific branch and above all in the first of all sciences, the science of freedom, equal rights, and self government." Responding to his welcome at Harvard, Lafayette recalled his visit forty years earlier. "The great improvements which have been made here during the interval are striking evidences of the tendency of liberal political institutions to promote the progress of civilization and learning." At Princeton, he recalled "the illustrious college which in diffusing knowledge and liberal sentiments, has greatly contributed to turn those successes to the advantage of public liberty." At the University of Virginia he offered the toast: "May it more and more diffuse through every part of mankind the principles, the feelings, and the benefits of true knowledge, general philanthropy, and unalloyed republicanism." To the students of Dickenson College, Lafayette suggested, "Upon the youth of the United States, we depend for the preservation of the free institutions and republican spirit. . . ."[38]

Following the pattern of his remarks to the New York Society of Cincinnati, Lafayette expressed fraternal feelings as he met the assemblies of the society from other states. To the Massachusetts chapter, he spoke of those no longer present and then added:

> While we mourn together for those we have lost, while I find a consolation in the sight of their relations and friends, it is to me a delightful gratification to recognize my surviving companions of our revolutionary army—that army so brave, so virtuous, so united by mutual confidence and affection. That we have been the faithful soldiers of independence, freedom, and equality, those three essential requisites of national and personal dignity and happiness; that we have lived to see those sacred principles secured to this vast Republic, and cherished elsewhere by generous minds . . .

He reminded the New Jersey chapter, "This happy country is now in the full enjoyment of the invaluable benefits of those sacred rights of human nature for which we fought and bled, and we must not despair of their final triumph on the other side of the Atlantic." To the Pennsylvania chapter, he proclaimed, "We Soldiers of national independence and equal rights can-

38. ALG, cote 270, no. 90; the substance of Lafayette's remarks at Harvard are in Brandon, *Lafayette Guest of the Nation,* 1: 110; ALG cote 270, no. 106; Brandon, *Lafayette Guest of the Nation,* 2: 38; Ibid., 3: 239.

not but be particularly proud of those principles, the happy consequences of which we have lived to witness." In addition to recalling the memory of departed comrades, Lafayette reminded the South Carolina members, "We witness the blessings of independence, prosperity and self government, which have been the result of our glorious war. . . .[39]

A number of groups not represented in that first appearance in New York City later became favorite topics for addresses by Lafayette. These include interdenominational clergy gatherings. Lafayette offered a salute in Philadelphia to such a group who provided him as he expressed it:

> . . . an additional proof of the holy fraternity which, in this happy land, unites together the ministers of a gospel of liberty and equality. How can the republican principles be better supported than by pastors who to their own eminent virtues join the inappreciable advantage of being the free elective choice of their respective congregations.

Similarly he commended the clergy of Savannah: "America, sir, has given an example of true religious freedom to old Europe, where a limited toleration was alone admitted. So I will observe in religious, as well as political societies election by the people is the best pledge of mutual confidence and regard."[40]

In addition to words, Lafayette sometimes expressed his views with public gestures. Lafayette's public embraces of and handshakes with African Americans drew attention across America, especially in southern states. The most famous of these was his encounter in Richmond with the former slave and Revolutionary war spy James Armistead (who had changed his name to James Armistead Lafayette). As the *Richmond Enquirer* reported in October 1824, "A black man . . . was recognized by him in the crowd, called to him by name, and taken into his embrace. Such is the goodness, the liberality, and true greatness of the man. . . ."[41] The incident was not isolated: in August 1824 at the State House in Boston Lafayette had to the general approval of the crowd embraced a black man named John Harrison who had been

39. Brandon, *Lafayette Guest of the Nation*, 1: 119-20; Ibid., 2: 45, 77; Brandon, *A Pilgrimage of Liberty*, 69.

40. ALG, cote 270, no. 17; *An Account of Lafayette in Savannah*, 43; Lafayette's draft remarks in Savannah are at ALG, cote 270, no. 54. Lafayette seems to have enjoyed these humorous strikes at the term "Holy Alliance."

41. Brandon, *Lafayette Guest of the Nation*, 1: 111. The account from the October 29, *Richmond Enquirer* is reproduced in ibid., 3: 121.

a servant of Samuel Breck when Lafayette had resided there. A Virginia newspaper reported that while receiving a line of well-wishers in Philadelphia, Lafayette had heard a familiar sound. A black man named Robert got Lafayette's attention by his whistling salutes. According to the newspaper, Lafayette remembered him with a hearty public handshake and the remark, "You was that roguish boy that used to make castanets of the dry bones in the camp and disturb me in my marquee." In Columbia, South Carolina, Lafayette was approached by an enslaved black man named Pompey Fortune, whose owner, John Buchanan, had welcomed Lafayette when he first arrived in South Carolina in 1777. Lafayette not only shook his hand but ordered glasses of champagne for the two. In Savannah Lafayette met with a slave named Nelson, who had served Lafayette during the Revolution. The stories indicate that Lafayette recognized all these men and publicly embraced them.[42]

Yet Lafayette's actions were not aimed merely at an American audience. One of Lafayette's intentions in the tour was to provide an account of his reception in America and a report of the benefits of American republicanism in such a way as to encourage liberals in France and elsewhere in Europe. The reporting of Lafayette's travels in America, though limited by French censors, nevertheless provided a masterful example of journalists working around their obvious limitations. The first major article on Lafayette's arrival in America appeared on the front page of the liberal Paris newspaper *Constitutionnel* on October 3, 1824. Though it avoided quoting Lafayette's responses to the crowds and the dignitaries, it extensively quoted the welcome address by the mayor of Boston. In subsequent issues, the articles drew perilously close to the boundaries that censors would allow; they were allowed to include lists of toasts, lists of processions of dignitaries and ordinary citizens, generous details of arrangements and the phrases written on objects (for example, the triumphal arches) such as "Lafayette, companion of Washington and friend of liberty."[43] Eventually the words of Lafayette slowly began to appear in French liberal newspapers. *Le Courrier Français*

42. The Philadelphia story from the *National Gazette* was reprinted in the *Alexandria Gazette*, October 7, 1824. The Columbia story is first printed by Maurice Augustus Moore in his "Reminiscences of York," which first appeared serially in a local newspaper after the Civil War, Elmer Otis Parker, ed., *Reminiscences of York by Dr. Maurice Moore* (Greenville, South Carolina: A Press, Inc., 1981), 95-96. For a contemporary newspaper account of the Savannah event, see Brandon, *Pilgrimage of Liberty*, 106.

43. *Constitutionnel*, October 3, 19, and 23; November 6, 29; December 2; "Lafayette compagnon de Washington et ami de la liberté."

published the text of his remarks to the mayor of Baltimore in its November 13 issue: "Sir, I admire with delight, your improvements, your prosperity, your patriotic troops. . . ."[44] After first trying to ignore the events, the conservative newspaper *Drapeau Blanc* finally responded with a charge that the American reception of Lafayette was a hostile act against Europe and nearly a declaration of war against the Holy Alliance. The *Constitutionnel* countered by printing yet stronger statements from Lafayette, for example, his January 1, 1825, toast to Congress, "Perpetual union among the United States; it has saved us in our times of danger; it will save the world."[45]

Lafayette's admirers were taken aback by the boldness of many of his criticisms of the royalist French government throughout the American tour. Many feared for his fate when he returned to his native country. Among the latter was the president of the United States, John Quincy Adams. As Lafayette was preparing for his return, Adams sought to extract a promise from the old veteran to lower his level of involvement in European controversies. Though Lafayette responded with a perfunctory agreement, Adams suspected his real intentions. On August 28 Adams wrote in his diary, "Conversation with General La Fayette after breakfast. I take every opportunity to dissuade him from having any participation in revolutionary projects in France. He says he will go quietly to La Grange; that he is sixty-eight years old, and must leave revolutions to young men. But there is fire beneath the cinders."[46]

* * *

Upon his return to France in October 1825, Lafayette resumed his role as a prominent leader of the liberals in the years before the Revolution of 1830. A few days before his arrival, the *Constitutionnel* advertised the appearance of a French translation of an American biography of Lafayette, one

44. Brandon, *Lafayette Guest of the Nation*, 2: 127. The Paris newspaper rendered the phrase: "Monsieur, j'admire avec bonheur vos progrès immenses, votre prospérité, vos troupes patriotiques, vos monuments." Lafayette retained copies of these French newspapers (NIC: Lafayette Collection).

45. The liberal reaction to the attack by the *Drapeau Blanc* appears in the *Constitutionnel* of February 3, 1825. Lafayette's toast (Brandon, *Lafayette Guest of the Nation*, 3: 181) was translated into French in the newspaper as "A l'union perpetuelle des Etats-Unis; elle nous a sauvé dans des momens de danger; elle sauvera le monde" (*Constitutionnel*, February 7, 1825).

46. Charles Francis Adams, ed., *Memoirs of John Quincy Adams: comprising portions of his diary from 1795 to 1848*, 12 vols. (Philadelphia: J. B. Lippincott & Co., 1874-77), 7: 49.

of many that had appeared in the United States during the tour. A second edition appeared soon after. This was followed in 1826 by an anonymously published work on Lafayette's 1824-25 American tour that appeared in Paris in four parts. Attributed to Charles Ogé Barbaroux and Alexandre Lardier, the 364-page account of the tour included a map of Lafayette' movements throughout the United States and generous excerpts from his speeches. These publications in France appear to have reflected a more relaxed censorship policy since the time of Lafayette's departure from France in 1824. The famous account of the trip by Lafayette's secretary Levasseur would not appear until the end of the summer of 1829 when Lafayette was ending yet another tour. During this last tour Lafayette would use the same words and symbols as during his American tour of 1824-25 to promote liberal causes in his native country, but this time the French government under Charles X was not receptive to either his actions or his words.[47]

As the summer of 1829 approached, Lafayette initially had decided to travel across France in connection with a visit to his birthplace in Auvergne. By the beginning of July, however, his initial plan for a simple family reunion was becoming more complicated. He found himself busily arranging appearances along the way for specific dates. His son Georges was already at the family estate in southern France, Chavaniac, making arrangements for his father's arrival. In the middle of frenetic activity the son confessed to a close friend, "My father is my father."[48]

To circulate his speeches among the French population, Lafayette returned to the same means he had used in America to publicize his ideas, local newspapers, to publish the text of his speeches and the events sur-

47. *Histoire du Général La Fayette* (Paris, 1825); *Constitutionnel*, October 1, 1824; the translation appears to have been the work of a Monsieur Dubergier who had found a career in Paris in the 1820s translating English language books; *Voyage du Général Lafayette aux Etats-Unis d'Amérique, en 1824 et 1825* (Paris, 1826). The *Constitutionnel* announced the publication of the final part of the book in its May 5 1826 issue. The authors' autograph presentation copy to George-Washington Lafayette is in the Division of Rare and Manuscript Collections, Carl A. Kroch Library, Cornell University.

48. Lafayette to James Barbour, July 8, 1829, Manuscript 5, 7C 6933: 1, Virginia Historical Society, Richmond, Virginia; [Mme George Washington Lafayette] to her husband, July 12, 1829, NIC: Lafayette Collection, Box 65, folder 6; ". . . mon père est mon père . . ." George Washington Lafayette to M. Bonne-Chevant, July 19, 1829, Manauscrit 1473 J, Archives départementales de la Haute-Loire, Le Puy-en-Velay, France.

rounding them. Over the next few days, Lafayette would also support the publication of individual pamphlets for specific cities to cover the events and major speeches of the entire tour.

The details of his first major event, a July 28 banquet at Clermont, appeared on the front page of the local liberal newspaper *L'Ami de la Charte* along with a series of toasts that took the role of mini-speeches from the other participants and concluded with patriotic songs. Lafayette urged his audience, "Today, sirs, we march progressively, I hope, but slowly I must admit, towards our constant goal, national liberty."[49]

On July 30, Lafayette reached Brioude, where his carriage was surrounded by a cavalry escort of young men and was addressed by his hosts with a reference to the recent American tour: "The one whose long career has been only a generous devotion to the cause of peoples and liberty, can walk only surrounded by homage and love; also, General, on whatever continent, on whatever coast carries your steps, your travels are only triumphal journeys—glorious triumph! These are the acclamations of free men and the popularity of virtue."[50] A quarter league from Brioude, Lafayette found a triumphal arch over the road, just as he had encountered in various American cities.[51] At the ensuing banquet Lafayette offered a toast for past and future, "To the town and arrondissement of Brioude! My eyes were opened there in the middle of usurpations of privilege and arbitrariness; may they, before they close, see my land in the full possession of all its rights, in the full use of its benefits of pure and complete liberty!"[52]

49. "Aujourd'hui, Messieurs, nous marchons progressivement, j'espère, mais lentement, il faut l'avouer, vers notre but constant la liberté nationale," *L'Ami de la Charte: Journal du Puy-de-Dome, de la Haute-Loire et du Cantal*, July 29, 1829. Lafayette wrote to his daughter Virginie the following day, "Vessiere has made a very pretty song that you will find surely in his *Ami de la Charte*." Lafayette to Virginie, July 28-29, 1829, ALG, cote 370.

50. "Celui dont la longue carrière n'a été qu'un dévouement généreux à la cause des peoples et de la liberté, ne peut marcher qu'entouré d'hommages et d'amour; aussi, Général, sur quelque continent, de quelque coté que se portent vos pas, vos voyages ne sont que des courses triomphales; triomphe glorieux! Ce sont les acclamations d'hommes libres et la popularité de la vertu." *Arrivée du Général Lafayette dans l'arrondissement de Brioude* (Clermont-Ferrand: Imprimerie J. Vassière, 1829), 2.

51. For an example of these triumphal arches on Lafayette's 1824-25 American tour, see Wayne Craven, "Origins of Sculpture in America: Philadelphia, 1785-1830," *American Art Journal* 9 (November 1977), 29.

52. "A la ville et à l'arrondissement de Brioude! Mes yeux s'y sont ouverts au milieu des

On August 1 at Issoire, there was another banquet and more speeches. Again, the Clermont newspaper *Ami de la Charte* published the speeches and toasts. After a few days at Chavaniac, Lafayette set out for Le Puy. There the *Ami de la Charte* reported a banquet of 150 persons on August 11. At the banquet Lafayette's unpublished toast was, "To the majesty of the people, immortal as it is, let us bow down before it and swear to be ready always to defend the rights and national interests at all times, in all places, at any price."[53]

From there Lafayette continued on his trip to Grenoble, the residence of his granddaughter's in-laws, the Périers, where the mayor presented him with a civic crown of silver-covered oak leaves, paid for by citizen contributions of fifty centimes each.[54] On August 16 Lafayette was toasted at a banquet there. "To the one who was at every time the sustainer of our liberties, of those liberties that we shall defend with as much constancy as they now seem to be gravely menaced."[55] But the monarchy was not making Lafayette's trip an easy one. Lafayette reported to his daughter-in-law that the mayor of Grenoble had originally wanted to close the city gate to the population and forbid their entry with a Swiss regiment if only the prefect there had not denied the request.[56]

---

usurpations du privilège et de l'arbitraire; puissent-ils, avant de se fermer, voir mon pays en pleine possession de tous ses droits, en pleine jouissance des bienfaits d'une pure et complète liberté." *Arrivée du Général Lafayette*, 8.

53. "A la majesté du people, immortelle comme lui,—inclinons nous respectueusement devant elle, et jurons lui d'etre toujours prets à défendre les droits et les intérets nationaux en tout tems, en tous lieux, à tout prix." Lafayette's speeches and toasts at Le Puy (in the handwriting of his son) are in NIC: Lafayette Collection, Box 101, folder 6. The toasts were not communicated to the publisher and did not appear in the pamphlet of the event, (*Arrivée du Général Lafayette au Puy le 11 aout 1829* [Le Puy: Imprimerie de Clet, 1829]).

54. In 1957, the civic crown was still in the hand of the Lafayette family, comte and comtesse d'Harcourt, Chantal de Tourtier Bonazzi and others, eds., *La Fayette: Exposition organisée par les Archives Nationales* (Paris: Hotel de Rohan, 1957), items 432, 433, p. 141.

55. "Au général Lafayette! À celui qui fut dans tous les temps le soutient de nos libertés, de ces libertés que nous défendrons avec d'autant plus de constance qu'elles semblent maintenant plus gravement menacées." *Banquet offert au Général Lafayette, le 18 aout 1829, par les citoyens de Grenoble* (Lyon: Imprimerie de Brunet, [1829]), 2.

56. Lafayette to Emilie de Lafayette, August 21, 1829, Paris, Archives Nationales, 252 AP 3, pièce 160. Lafayette repeated the story about the mayor of Grenoble in his letter to his daughter Virginie, August 22, ALG, cote 370.

As a deputation from Lyon made its way to Vizille to meet Lafayette and invite him to their city, the mayor of Lyon was busy informing the Minister of the Interior about the plans for Lafayette's reception there. From Vizille, Lafayette took the opportunity to write to his secretary, Levasseur, during his recent American tour to congratulate him on the publication of his account of that American tour and to suggest that he would provide Levasseur with some advice for future editions. Lafayette then turned his attention in the letter to the current French tour. "The details of our trip . . . have been given in the *Ami de la Charte*, The *Precurseur*, and the *Courrier Français*." He urged Levasseur to forward reports to his American friend Peter Duponceau who had habitually forwarded news about Lafayette to Philadelphia newspapers to be dispersed through other papers around the United States. Lafayette also indicated that his current secretary Berger would help him collect those materials before the packet boat for America sailed.[57]

As Lafayette's tour approached the major city of Lyon, the monarchy was preparing to take precautions. The mayor of Lyon issued an ordinance on August 28, forbidding serenades, charivaris, and acclamations held on public streets. The local liberal newspaper, the *Precurseur*, reported that the ordinance had the exact opposite effect, emboldening the population to redouble their efforts for Lafayette's reception. The paper openly accused the government of trying to impede the reception for Lafayette. Actually the Minister of the Interior La Bourdonnaye had sent such an instruction to the comte de Brosses, prefect of the Rhone, on August 28.[58]

57. "Les details de notre passage sur la route de Chavaniac et de Vizille ont été donnés dans l'Ami de la Charte, le Precurseur, et le Courier français," Lafayette to Levasseur, August 28, 1829, Stuart Jackson Collection, Box 2 [uncatalogued], Beinecke Library, Yale University, New Haven, Connecticut. A review of Levasseur's work appeared in the *Tribune des départemens* on September 16, 1829, and noted:

"La France a observé avec trop d'attention les effets de la reconnaissance républicaine des citoyens de l'Union, elle a suivi avec trop d'intéret tous les détails de ce memorable evénement, pour que nous entreprenions de les réproduire ici, surtout au moment où notre pays vient de prouver d'une manière si éclatante qu'il a se profiter de l'exemple donné par les Etats-unis, et que une admiration pour le plus illustre représentant de la liberté dans les deux mondes n'est pas moins vive que la leur. Remarquons toutefois que dans l'un et l'autre hemisphère, à Boston comme à Lyon, les discours addresses à Lafayette ont exprimé avec égale franchise le bien qu'il a fait ou voulu faire aux Américains et aux Français.

58. The report from the *Precurseur* of August 1 appeared in the Paris-based *Tribune des départemens* on 6 September and in the Clermont *Ami de la Charte* on 2 September. La Bourdonnaye to Prefect of the Rhone, August 28, 1829, Ms. 2323, fols. 26-27,

As news of the conflict between royal officials and the Lafayette entourage reached Paris, the *Globe* newspaper there published an article titled "General Lafayette and the Ministry" that was reprinted across the region.

> What's happening in France? Why these devices of festivities, these triumphal arches, these mountains crowned with torches? What impels these populations filled with joy and gratitude? Is it the king who travels, following some great widespread benefit or some great misfortune undone? No, it is a simple citizen. But this simple citizen is Lafayette.[59]

The *Tribune des départemens* threw down a challenge: "Now, counterrevolutionaries of every name and every rank, if you dare, enter the countryside, tear up the Charter . . . !"[60] Reports circulated that in some towns even the local mayors had participated in the ceremonies, especially at Vizille and Vienne. Again reminding its readers of Lafayette's American exploits, the *Tribune des départemens*, proclaimed, "It is more than a half century since the shores of Charleston saw him full of youth, ardor, and hope; his flag was that of liberty, his adversaries [were] oppressors; Brandywine saw his generous blood run, and Yorktown was witness of his victory." The editors further recalled his service in the French Revolution, his proposal for the Declaration of Rights and his service in the National Guard. "Who," they asked, "calls him a usurper?"[61]

Bibliothèque Municipale, Lyon, France. The following day, similar letters went out to the prefects of Haute-Loire and the Ardèche, F7 6720, dossier 12, Archives Nationales, Paris, France.

59. "Qui se passé-t-il donc en France? Pourquoi ces appareils de fetes, ces arcs de triomphe, ces montagnes couronnées de feux? Où se precipitant ces populations ardentes de joie et de reconnaissance? Est-il le roi qui voyage, après quelque grand bienfait répandu ou quelque grand Malheur réparé? Non, c'est un simple citoyen. Mais ce simple citoyen, c'est Lafayette." The article appeared in the *Ami de la Charte* on 19 September.

60. "Maintenant, contre-révolutionnaires de tous noms et de tous rangs, entrez, si vous l'osez, en campagne, déchirez la Charte. . . ." *Tribune des départemens*, September 13, 1829.

61. "Il y a plus d'un demi-siècle que les rivages de Charles-Town le virent plein de jeunesse, d'ardeur et d'ésperance; son drapeau était celui de la liberté; ses adversaries, des oppresseurs. Brandy-Wine vit écouler son sang généreux, at York-Town fut témoin de sa victoire . . . qui l'appelle aujourd'hui un usurpateur?" Ibid., September 9. For Lafayette's relationship with the editor of this newspaper, Auguste Fabre, see

Lafayette's visit to Lyon was the high point of the tour, lasting several days. His arrival into the city on September 5 was led by three hundred mounted young men, musicians on horseback, and several vehicles. The crowd was numbered by royal officials at 25,000; liberal newspapers numbered it at 60,000. In his banquet speech the following night he launched an attack on the double vote, reminding his listeners that already by terms of the Charter for every one hundred Frenchmen of eligible age, only one could exercise that right. In conclusion he offered his audience this toast: "To the department of the Rhone and the city of Lyon, ancient center of industry, courageous enemy of oppression! May its liberty, its dignity, its prosperity be solidly founded on the full enjoyment of the natural and social rights that it invokes in all times."[62]

Rumors that Lafayette might appear in Dijon led the mayor of that city to preemptively forbid serenades in the streets in his honor, an order that was posted on the street corners.[63] But this order was to no effect because Lafayette was on his way back to Paris. To Levasseur, Lafayette wrote from the calm of his country estate LaGrange that issues of the Paris newspapers

---

Lafayette's letter of introduction of him to Casimir Périer, September 19, Papiers de la famille Périer, 11J42 cote 7, Archives départementales de l'Isère, Gernoble, France.

Because Faure Finant, the mayor of Vizille, had participated in the Lafayette ceremonies, he was quickly removed from office (*Tribune des départemens*, September 27, 1829). The text of Lafayette's September 26 letter consoling the mayor on his removal appears in [George Washington Lafayette and others], eds., *Mémoires, correspondance et manuscrits du Général Lafayette,* 6 vols. (Paris: H. Fournier ainé, 1837-1838), 6: 336-37.

62. "Au department du Rhone et à la ville de Lyon, antique métropole d'industrie, courageuse ennemie de l'oppression. Puissent sa liberté, sa dignité, sa prosperité, etre solidement fondée sur la pleine jouissance des droits nationals et sociaux qu'elle invoque dans tous les temps." *Tribune des départemens*, September 9 and 12; *Le Presurseur: Journal contitutionnel de Lyon et du* Midi, September 6 (F7 6790, dossier 12, pièce 58, Archives Nationales, Paris, France); Ami *de la Charte*, September 10, 19. The September 5 report of events sent by the mayor of Lyon Lacroix Laval to his superior suggests that Lafayette's entourage of horsemen numbered 103 (F 7 6720, dossier 12, pièce 68, Archives Nationales, Paris, France).

An account of Lafayette's appearance at the Masonic lodge in Lyon was printed and sent to Parisian masons (Loge du Parfait Silence de Lyon to Loge des Trinosophes de Paris, September 24, 1829, Stuart Jackson Collection, box 4 (uncatalogued), Beinecke Library, Yale University, New Haven, Connecticut.

63. *Ami de la Charte*, 23 September. The full text of the September 9 order appeared in *Tribune des départemens*, September 14.

Le Constitutionnel, *Le Courrier*, and the *Journal des débats* reporting the banquet at Lyon had been halted in the mails. Lafayette urged Levasseur to convey this news to the editors of the Paris papers for further articles. To his son, the general noted that the royalist (or as he termed them "counterrevolutionary") newspapers were attacking his trip, and the liberal newspapers were "full of good things for the trip and the travelers." He also acknowledged to his son that Levasseur's new book on the American tour was selling well. Appearing about the time of Lafayette's French tour, no doubt readers would be able to compare the two and—as Lafayette hoped—judge the benefits of an enlightened and progressive republic for themselves.[64]

That same day Lafayette sent his old Philadelphia friend Duponceau a bundle of liberal and royalist newspapers filled with their reactions to the French voyage along with his suggestion: "If you judge it useful to publish the speeches of your old friend, namely his responses at Lyon, please translate them carefully. . . . National firmness will triumph from it, and I am very happy to think that a family trip . . . has provided the occasion to manifest French patriotism."[65] Even against a hostile and mobilized French royalist bureaucracy, Lafayette found ways to spread his message and to encourage and activate public opposition to the Restoration regime. That tour during the summer of 1829 would in turn set the stage for the events of the sum-

64. Lafayette to Levasseur, September 14 [1829], Stuart Jackson Collection, Box 2 (uncatalogued), Beinecke Library, Yale University, New Haven, Connecticut. Lafayette also reported the action to his son. Yet, as he further noted, the events in Lyons had been fully reported in the *Ami de la Charte* and *Le Précurseur*, which had not been intercepted; "Les publications liberales sont pleines de bonté pour le voiage et les voyageurs." Lafayette to G. W. Lafayette, September 15, Pierpont Morgan Library, New York City, New York.

65. "Si vous jugez utile de publier les discours de votre vieux ami, nommément ses réponses à Lyon, je vous prie d'en soigner la traduction. . . . La fermeté nationale en triomphera, et je suis heureux de penser qu'un voyage de famille . . . a fourni une occasion de manifester le patriotisme français" (Lafayette to [Duponceau], September 15, 1829, Manuscripts 2 L1314a2, Virginia Historical Society, Richmond, Virginia. Lafayette wrote to a visiting Virginian on September 26, "I have been much obliged to my editorial friends, particularly Mr. Ritchie, for the care they have taken to publish such informations as may keep me under the inspection of American fellow citizens whose approbation of my sentiments and conduct you know to be so very essential to me" (L to unknown, copy in ALG, cote 259B). Thomas Ritchie was editor of the *Richmond Enquirer*. Reports of Lafayette's visit to Lyon appeared in American newspapers in late October such as the (Washington) *National Intelligencer* (October 24) and *The* (Savannah) *Georgian* (October 24).

mer of 1830.[66]

* * *

In conclusion, throughout these three "tours," 1784, 1824-25, and finally 1829, Lafayette had increased his understanding and mastery of the importance of public performance and publicity to his and what he considered the American Revolution's original agenda. The 1784 tour had begun as a simple "triumphal tour," an opportunity to recall good times with old friends and comrades, but when it was underway Lafayette found another opportunity to attend to the new challenges for the future of the United States. By the 1824-25 tour, though the number of Lafayette's wartime American friends had dwindled to a few, their children and grandchildren knew of his accomplishments, and he found a new audience for his words. This time Lafayette came with the intention of reminding Americans why the war had been fought and urging that they, as heirs of the revolution, had a continuing duty to advance the republican and liberal causes at home and abroad. Back in France, Lafayette took the opportunity in 1829 of a business and family trip to Auvergne to send a similar message on a third tour to a new generation of Frenchmen. Lafayette's speeches and toasts during these three tours over a forty-one year period reveal a consistent but developing agenda. His vocabulary, of course, included those terms that had been at the core of the American Revolution and the French Revolution of 1789, but by the 1820s Lafayette's vocabulary was expanding to include the social and political agenda of a new generation. His American experience reminded him of the importance of a free French press. Lafayette's political vision was continuing to expand, and to take on the transatlantic perspective that was becoming possible in the increasingly intertwined Atlantic world.

66. David H. Pickney in his masterful *The French Revolution of 1830* reports a memorandum by Polignac of September 10, 1829, in which he "declared his dissatisfaction with the power of the middle class in France, the abuses of the press, . . . and expressed his wish that the doors of the Chamber of Deputies might somehow be closed to 'mediocre men driven by turbulent and revolutionary passions,'" but Pinckney does not indicate what event(s) drove Polignac to make this statement *The French Revolution of 1830* (Princeton University Press, 1972), 10-11. Bertier de Sauvigny briefly notes the tour in the "southeast" as a manifestation of liberal protest, G. De Bertier de Sauvigny, *La Restauration* (Paris: Flammarion, 1955), 427. Pamela Pilbeam's study does not mention the tour at all in discussing the background to the Revolution of 1830, Pamela Pilbeam, *The 1830 Revolution in France* (New York: St. Martin's Press, 1991).

6 Culture Clash in Louisiana's Territorial Period: The Marquis de Lafayette's American Land Grants

Todd Bourque

On August 19, 1792, the Prussian army, fighting against the French Convention, detained the Marquis de Lafayette in Belgium and charged him with fomenting the revolution that led to the beheading of King Louis XVI. After three years in prison at Olmütz, Austria, and two years exiled from France, Lafayette finally returned to his chateau, LaGrange, in 1799. Although considered by many in France as a champion of liberty and a hero of the 1789 French Revolution, Lafayette remained an illegal émigré, subject to immediate arrest in his native country until March 1, 1800, when, in need of reconciling the political factions in France, Napoleon Bonaparte reinstated Lafayette's citizenship in exchange for Lafayette's retirement from public life. The five years removed from his finances left Lafayette with a mounting debt. Lafayette's wife, Marie-Adrienne-Françoise de Noailles, who orchestrated the reclamation of Lafayette's French citizenship, titles, and property, continued lobbying for the return of all the Lafayette family assets. Adrienne's efforts provided subsistence and kept the family out of bankruptcy, but still fell short of paying off Lafayette's debts. Lafayette's own desire to remain loyal to the original principles of the French Revolution—liberty, equality, and fraternity—did not help matters. Indeed, Lafayette's refusal to support the Napoleon government cost the family additional hardships including the public auction of their lands in Brittany.[1] More revenue would be needed for the family to regain the same comfortable and manageable financial position that they enjoyed before Lafayette's imprisonment. Lafayette's connection to the United States and his unique identity as a powerful symbol for French-American friendship, suddenly assumed a new importance as

1. An Officer in the Late Army, *A Complete History of the Marquis de Lafayette, Major General in the Army of the United States of America, In the War of the Revolution; Embracing an Account of his Late Tour Through the United States to the Time of His Departure, September, 1825* (Hartford, CT: S. Andrus and Son, 1846), 276-80.

his only hope of restoring his fortune and influence. But this moment would also mark the beginning of a complex and fraught relationship between Lafayette and his land holdings in the Americas, especially those in Louisiana.

Arriving in France in April 1802, James Monroe answered Lafayette's financial prayers. Appointed by President Thomas Jefferson as a special envoy, Monroe was in France to negotiate the purchase of the Louisiana Territory, recently regained from Spain in 1800 by Napoleon Bonaparte. Monroe informed Lafayette that Congress had recently set aside land in the Ohio River Valley for veterans of the American Revolution who received land warrants for service in the Continental Army. As a general under George Washington's command and an instrumental figure in the siege of Yorktown in 1781 that ended the American Revolution, Lafayette qualified to receive some of this land. On March 3, 1803, Congress issued land warrants to Lafayette totaling 11,520 acres north of the Ohio River and above the mouth of the Kentucky River.[2] When Lafayette asked if the land could be used to generate revenue, Monroe offered to use the land warrants as collateral to guarantee a loan for Lafayette. Indeed, Monroe personally brokered the loan from Francis Baring in London totaling 250,000 livres, which retired Lafayette's remaining debts. One obstacle, congressional approval for the Louisiana Purchase, would stop Lafayette from exercising his warrants in the Ohio River Valley.

Indeed, three U.S. presidents, from 1802-1924, would become personally involved in Lafayette's land claims in Louisiana. Lafayette would be the only veteran of the American Revolution named as a land warrant holder in the Congressional record. This unprecedented personal attention given to Lafayette in appreciation for his service to American independence bred discontent among Louisiana's property owners whose colonial land claims thwarted the federal government's attempt to secure prime real estate for Lafayette. Even before the U.S. Senate approved the Louisiana Purchase, President Thomas Jefferson had already offered the Louisiana governorship to Lafayette. In an 1802 letter, Jefferson expressed the need for the French general to maintain peace among Louisiana's predominantly francophone inhabitants. "I would prefer your presence to an army of 10,000 men to assure the tranquility of the country. . . . The old French inhabitants would immediately attach themselves to you and to the United States. You would

2. *An Act to revive and continue in force, an act in addition to an act intituled "An act in addition to an act regulating the grants of land appropriated for Military Services and for the Society of the United Brethren for propagating the Gospel among the Heathen," and for other purposes*, 7th Cong., 2nd sess., chap. XXX, stat. II, sec. 4 (March 3, 1803).

annul the efforts of the foreign agitators who are arriving in droves."[3] Jefferson had ample reason to suspect a difficult transfer of power over Louisiana from France to the United States. Just three years prior, Louisianans were celebrating the retrocession of the colony from Spain back to France following the October 1, 1800, Treaty of San Ile Defonso. Predominantly French in culture and ancestry, Louisianans would learn of the sale of the colony to the United States simultaneously with Pierre Clement de Laussat, the French prefect sent to Louisiana to receive the colony from Spain and to reestablish French authority.

Although his tenure in Louisiana was short-lived, Laussat made note of the colonists' reactions to the transfer of Louisiana to the United States and the inhabitants' views of their new fellow Americans, based on their limited experiences with American merchants in New Orleans and frontiersmen further north along the Mississippi River: "The Americans . . . introduced the strictness of their laws and exactness of their customs. For two months they had been apprehending and imprisoning debtors. Each one [American] turned over in his mind a little plan of speculation. . . . They were invading Louisiana as the holy tribes invaded the land of Canaan."[4] Louisiana's population had many reasons to view Anglo-Americans with wariness. They had no prior experiences with republican forms of government, nor U.S. laws, and therefore were at a disadvantage, particularly in judicial proceedings concerning disputes with Anglo-Americans. They tended to see such things as serving on juries and electing officials as a nuisance rather than a civic duty. For nearly one hundred years, Louisiana colonists relied on the patriar-

3. George-Washington Lafayette et Gilbert Motier, Marquis de Lafayette, *Mémoires, Correspondence et Manuscrits du Général Lafayette, publiés par sa famille*, vol. II (Paris: H. Fournier, 1837), 224.

4. Pierre Clément de Laussat, *Memoirs of My Life*, Agnes-Josephine Pastwa trans. (Baton Rouge: Louisiana State University Press, 1978), 100, 103. The tensions between Louisianians and Anglo-Americans during Louisiana's territorial period are legendary. For more information, see: Jared W. Bradley, "W.C.C. Claiborne and Spain: Foreign Affairs under Jefferson and Madison, 1801-1811," *Louisiana History: The Journal of the Louisiana Historical Association* XII (Autumn, 1971): 297-314; Peter J. Kastor, "'Motives of Peculiear Urgency': Local Diplomacy in Louisiana, 1803-1821," *The William and Mary Quarterly* 58 (October, 2001), 819-48; George Dargo, *Jefferson's Louisiana: Politics and the Clash of Legal Traditions* (Cambridge, MA, 1975); Alexander DeConde, *This Affair of Louisiana* (Baton Rouge: LSU Press, 1976); Paul E. Hoffman, ed., *The Louisiana Purchase and Its Peoples: Perspectives from the New Orleans Conference* (New Orleans, 1970).

chal benevolence of a monarch and his colonial representatives, and felt no need to take an active part in government, nor to overly concern themselves with participation in the crafting or execution of laws.

The new American officials held suspicious feelings towards the outgoing Spanish and French officials and the territorial inhabitants as a whole. In a January 2, 1804, letter to Secretary of State James Madison, Claiborne characterized the remaining Spanish and French government officials as having "scarcely a nerve not wounded by corruption."[5] On January 10, Claiborne acknowledged his fear of establishing a republican form of government among inhabitants he deemed "unfit for representative government."[6] Citing the continued partiality to the French regime, and the reliance of the larger whole on the wealthy and educated few for governance, Claiborne believed that Congress would do well to govern the territory until education and basic understanding of the United States' form of government could reduce the possibility of reverting back to an oligarchy. Indeed, both Laussat and the Spanish representative for the retrocession, Marques de Casa Calvo, would remain in Louisiana, as late as July 1804 for Laussat and 1806 for Casa Calvo, fomenting and encouraging anti-American sentiments and awaiting instructions from abroad in the hope of retaking the colony for their respective countries.[7] Knowing the sensitive nature of the situation in Louisiana with respect to maintaining peace among the inhabitants and Anglo-Americans, Jefferson waited for Lafayette's answer, which did not arrive until October 1, 1804.

As further inducement, Jefferson transferred Lafayette's Ohio land warrants to the Louisiana territory—specifically on the Isle of Orleans, land which Jefferson believed would prove valuable. Despite all attempts at persuasion, Lafayette declined the offer to govern the largest single U.S. territory. Having just restored his family name and estate in France, and regained hold on his properties and finances, Lafayette longed to retire from public life in his native country.[8] Jefferson, in need of an immediate substitution,

5. Rowland, Dunbar, ed., *Official Letter books of W. C. C. Claiborne, 1801-1816,* vol. 1 (Jackson: Mississippi State Department of Archives and History, 1917), 323.

6. Ibid., 329.

7. Rowland, *Official Letter books of W.C.C. Claiborne,* 2:347-48.

8. An Officer, *A Complete History of the Marquis de Lafayette,* 300-301; Randolph, Thomas Jefferson, ed., *Memoirs, Correspondence, and Private Papers of Thomas Jefferson, Late President of the United States,* vol. III (London: Henry Colburn and Richard Bentley, 1829), 22, 99.

appointed former Mississippi territorial governor, and then commissioner overseeing the transfer of Louisiana from France to the United States, William C.C. Claiborne, to serve as the territory's first governor. Jefferson included in his initial orders to Claiborne, "This office was originally destined for a person whose great services and established fame would have rendered him peculiarly acceptable to the nation at large."[9] The twenty-eight-year-old Claiborne, honored by the tremendous show of confidence in his abilities to handle such a monumental task, echoed Jefferson's sentiments towards Lafayette in his response, "But if Honest views, zealous and faithful attention to the duties intrusted [*sic*] to me will be accepted in lieu of Brilliant Abilities, I hope to retain that confidence of my Government, which at this time constitutes a principal Happiness of my life."[10] One can argue that Claiborne's reference is to Lafayette's unique ability to bring together various factions for a common cause as displayed during the initial machinations of the 1789 French Revolution.

Although Lafayette had declined the governorship, Congress approved the land warrant transfer, as requested by Jefferson, on March 27, 1804. In a July 18, 1804, letter to his close friend, Dr. Phillip Mazzei, Jefferson celebrated this achievement for its potential in relieving the financial woes of Lafayette,

> "The acquisition of Louisiana . . . has enabled us to do a handsome thing for Fayette. He had received a grant . . . North of the Ohio, worth, perhaps, a dollar an acre. We have obtained permission of Congress to locate it in Louisiana. Locations can be found adjacent to the city of New Orleans, in the island of New Orleans, and its vicinities, the value of which can not be calculated."[11]

Congress authorized Lafayette to survey and claim lands unoccupied, unimproved, and untitled in the territory of New Orleans in parcels no less than 1,000 acres.[12] This unprecedented privilege granted Lafayette, a non-

9. Randolph, Memoirs, Correspondence, and Private Papers of Thomas Jefferson, vol. IV, 26.

10. Rowland, ed., *Official Letter books of W. C. C. Claiborne,* I: 284.

11. Randolph, Thomas Jefferson, ed., *Memoirs, Correspondence, and Private Papers of Thomas Jefferson, Late President of the United States,* vol. III (London: Henry Colburn and Richard Bentley, 1829), 22.

12. *An Act supplementary to the act intituled "An act regulating the grants of land, and providing for the disposal of the lands of the United States, south of the state of Tennessee,"*

resident, to select the best lands in the vicinity of New Orleans disrupted the relations between residents and their new government, already strained by the 1803 purchase just twenty days after France reclaimed the colony. In all of the congressional statutes concerning land titles in the Orleans Territory, Lafayette is one of the few or perhaps the only individual identified by name. Additionally, the sections dealing with Lafayette's land grants are buried within statutes concerning the establishment of land and register's offices for Orleans Territory, job descriptions and salaries for the survey general and other land agents, and the incorporation of New Orleans. Indeed, the landmark statute of March 2, 1805, which divided the Louisiana Purchase into the territory of Orleans and the district of Louisiana, reiterated Lafayette's land authorization previously documented in 1804.[13]

Despite being French and enjoying the affection of the federal government, Lafayette's representatives met resistance among the francophone inhabitants of the Orleans Territory in their attempts to secure land in fulfillment of the Acts of Congress. On May 3, 1804, Louisiana Governor General William C. C. Claiborne wrote to President Jefferson, "My present impression is, that there would be no difficulty in locating the Land granted to General Fayette in situations the most eligible in lower Louisiana; perhaps the greater part of it, on the Island of New Orleans."[14] Claiborne took a personal interest in locating available lands by enlisting the advice of Charles Trudeau, former Surveyor General of Louisiana under the Spanish regime. However, from Claiborne's letter to Jefferson May 20, 1804, Trudeau offered no reassurance that Lafayette's warrants for 11, 520 acres could be exercised on the Isle of Orleans.[15] The best available large tracts, according to Trudeau, were found on the Red River at Rapides post, on the Atchafalaya River, and on the Iberville River and nearby bayous that would collectively total the specified acreage. Apparently unsatisfied, Claiborne attempted to secure a

---

8th Cong., 1st sess., chap. LXI, stat. I, sec. 14 (March 27, 1804).

13. *An act for ascertaining and adjusting the titles and claims to land within the territory of Orleans and the district of Louisiana*, 8th Cong., 2nd sess., chap. XXVI, stat. II, sec. 8 (March 2, 1805).

14. William C. C. Claiborne, Louisiana Territory, to Thomas Jefferson, Washington, D. C., May 3, 1804, Thomas Jefferson Papers, Library of Congress, available online at http://memory.loc.gov/ammem/index.html.

15. William C. C. Claiborne, Louisiana Territory, to Thomas Jefferson, Washington, D. C., May 20, 1804, Thomas Jefferson Papers, Library of Congress, available online at http://memory.loc.gov/ammem/index.html.

clear title to lands along the Carondelet Canal and Bayou St. John. However, the Mayor of New Orleans, Étienne de Boré, protested and produced documentation that the land, although vacant, belonged to the Commons of the City. Additionally, Mayor Boré reminded Claiborne that taking land from the City of New Orleans violated Claiborne's own promise to maintain the status quo as outlined in his letter to the people on December 20, 1803.[16] With this information, Claiborne altered his original synopsis, advocating parcels of land spread out in the territory of Orleans with a small area on the Isle reclaimed from the surrounding cypress swamps. However, even the one thousand acre minimum would prove difficult for Claiborne to secure.

These land troubles experienced by Lafayette's representatives in Louisiana in satisfying the general's land warrants on the Isle of Orleans exemplified the difficulty the United States would have reconciling Louisiana's colonial land policies with those of the new regime. Established in the Northwest Land Ordinance of May 1785 under the Articles of Confederation, the United States continued the practice of surveying new territories into townships prior to the sale of public lands.[17] Each township would equal six square miles, subdivided into sections of one square mile. Further subdivisions would follow the same squared pattern. The surveyed plats imposed a grid on the landscape with little consideration of geographical features. However, the plats could be resurveyed with relative ease, thus reducing the potential for land disputes either by natural occurrences—such as marker trees destroyed by storm, or riverbank erosion—or by manmade alterations—such as removal of markers.[18]

With the exception of the city of New Orleans, which was surveyed and laid out on a grid, colonial Louisiana's land practices differed greatly from those of the United States. Begun under the French and continued under the Spanish regime, land practices in the colony took into consideration the need for transportation, communication, and irrigation. Therefore, officials dispensed land with a specific waterfront distance, the side boundaries running perpendicular to the waterfront, and terminating at the next body of

16. Dunbar, ed., *Official Letter books of W. C. C. Claiborne,* 1: 309-310.

17. "An ordinance for ascertaining the mode of disposing of lands in the Western Territory," *Journals of the Continental Congress*, vol. 29: 923 (May 18, 1785).

18. For more information on the difference in land policies see: Coles, Jr., Harry L., "Applicability of the Public Land System to Louisiana," *The Mississippi Valley Historical Review,* 43 (June 1956), 39-58; and Paul Wallace Gates, "Private Land Claims in the South," *The Journal of Southern History,* 22 (May 1956), 183-204.

water, at another property boundary, or at a specific distance to satisfy a predetermined acreage. Defying any regularity, surveyors used stones, trees, or other landscape features as boundary markers, and numerous boundary disputes arose with the changes of the landscape over time. [19]

Following Trudeau's report as to the availability of public land on the Isle of Orleans, Jefferson expressed his concerns to Claiborne that Lafayette's land would be made up of worthless swamp and flood-prone land, which would undermine the intended act of gratitude. Perhaps sensing Claiborne's inability to reckon with his constituents, Jefferson sent word on May 26, 1805, that Armand Gabriel Allard Duplantier, a French-born cavalry officer and onetime aide-de-camp to Lafayette, who settled in Louisiana after the American Revolution, would serve as Lafayette's land agent in Louisiana, thus relieving Claiborne of any obligation.[20] Lafayette also granted James Monroe power of attorney over the Marquis's land interests in the United States.[21] After retiring from the French Army following the American Revolution, Duplantier had married Augustine Gerard of Pointe Coupée and settled with his family in the parish until her death from yellow fever in 1799. With his second wife, Constance Rochon Joyce, Duplantier moved to Magnolia Mound Plantation in Baton Rouge, Joyce's family inheritance.[22] It was his connection to Pointe Coupée, however, and its situation at the junction of the Red, Atchafalaya, and Mississippi Rivers, that influenced Duplantier's decision to exercise a portion of Lafayette's warrants in that parish. With a congressional supplement in 1806 to the March 2, 1805 Act, which reduced the minimum acreage from one thousand to five hundred, various small plots in the Territory of Orleans would be claimed for Lafayette.[23] The bulk of his warrants, however, would remain unclaimed until

19. For a visual appreciation of land plats along the Mississippi River, see Adrien Persac, "Norman's chart of the lower Mississippi River" (New York: J. H. Colton, 1858); and Morgan, "Plat, Field Notes, etc. of Lafayette warrant no. 4, February 11, 1808." Baton Rouge: Louisiana State University.

20. Thomas Jefferson, Washington, D. C., to William C. C. Claiborne, Louisiana Territory, May 26, 1805, Thomas Jefferson Papers, Library of Congress, available online at http://memory.loc.gov/ammem/index.html.

21. Stanislaus MurrayHamilton, ed., *The Writings of James Monroe Including a collection of his public and private papers and correspondence now for the first time printed*, vol. IV (New York: G. P. Putnam's Sons, 1900), 425, 429-32.

22. *A Dictionary of Louisiana Biography*, s. v. "Duplantier, Armand Gabriel Allard."

23. *An Act supplementary to the act intituled "An act for ascertaining and adjusting the*

the U.S. acquisition of Florida in 1821. Unlike American veterans who held similar land warrants for their service in the American Revolution, Lafayette's carried no expiration date.

Five years later, on February 11, 1808, Charles Morgan submitted a survey of one thousand acres in Pointe Coupée for the Marquis de Lafayette, verified and signed by Benedicte Van Pradelles, Register of the Land Office of the Eastern District of the Territory of Orleans, and R.W. Boyd, Surveyor General of Louisiana.[24] As a hybrid of both the Anglo-American and colonial Louisiana land surveying traditions, Lafayette's plat combines a partial riverfront access on the Mississippi River, with straight lines and ninety-degree angles in order to satisfy rectangular tracks of land along a highly irregular bend in the river. According to the description, the property markers consisted of "stakes," with coordinates and distances squared to a single corner of the plat on the edge of the river. Located on the Mississippi River approximately three miles south of its convergence with the Atchafalaya, Lafayette's first claim accounts for approximately one-fourth of the total land indicated in the Pointe Coupée Census of November 23, 1809. Since the remaining lands had not been located or surveyed, Lafayette's property is listed as "superficial," valued at $3.75 per arpent (equal to $.85 acre).[25]

From the 1809 census and other supporting documents, it appears that no improvements or cultivation occurred on Lafayette's claim. Armand Duplantier, Lafayette's land agent, is listed as the representative for Lafayette's landholding, but no slaves are enumerated for his property valuation. Although this absence does not provide definitive proof that the land remained unchanged, the circumstances surrounding the sale of Lafayette's Pointe Coupée land appear to suggest the same conclusion. Vincent Nolte, an international businessman with interests in New Orleans and friend of Lafayette, provides an account in his memoirs of Lafayette's land dealings in Pointe Coupée. According to Nolte, Lafayette approached him in Paris during the summer of 1824 requesting that he gather information about his land

titles and claims to land within the territory of Orleans and the district of Louisiana," 9th Cong., 1st sess., chap. XXXIX, stat. I, sec. 12 (April 21, 1806).

24. Charles Morgan, "Plat, Field Notes, etc. of Lafayette warrant no. 4, February 11, 1808," William Walter Survey Collection, Louisiana and Lower Mississippi Valley Collections, Hill Memorial Library, Baton Rouge: Louisiana State University.

25. Todd J. Bourque, "The Census of Point Coupée, 1809," *Louisiana History: The Journal of the Louisiana Historical Association*, XLVII (Spring 2006), 203-204, 221.

in the parish on his next trip to Louisiana.[26] The Barings of London, who allowed Lafayette to use some of his land warrants to secure a loan, agreed to a portion of Lafayette's Pointe Coupée holdings at the inflated price of $11.00 an acre in order to satisfy the loan amount. However, when Lafayette wrote to the Barings for an additional loan to fund his 1824 voyage to the United States, Alexander Baring refused the request, saying "we are not quite clear of an old scrape, and cannot plump into a fresh one." Shortly thereafter, Sir John Coghill, an English Baron living in Paris, approached Lafayette about buying four tracts of his Pointe Coupée parcel. Having learned of the sale price in the Baring transaction, Coghill expected a handsome return on the speculation. Coghill only learned of his error later on when the Barings failed to make any profit off the sale of their plot. Coghill paid 240,000 francs for his tracts, which the Pointe Coupée clerk of court registered on December 31, 1833, signed by President James Monroe who still held power of attorney over Lafayette's land warrants in the United States.[27] Coghill sold his parcel two years later, and they subsequently became C.D. Stewart's "Lake Side" and J.J. Pringle's "Torwood" plantations.[28]

Whether or not Lafayette ever received information regarding his Pointe Coupée lands remains unknown. Nolte failed to mention the results of his fact-finding mission. Although it is possible that Lafayette did see his lands from the steamboat Natchez on his Mississippi River voyage in 1825, Nolte, who accompanied Lafayette during the entire U.S. tour, makes no mention of it.[29] Auguste Levasseur, Lafayette's personal secretary who also accom-

26. Vincent Nolte, *Fifty years in both hemispheres or, Reminisces of the Life of a Former Merchant* (New York: Redfield, 1854), 306.

27. Nolte, *Fifty years in both hemispheres*, 306-307.

28. Adrien Persac, "Norman's chart of the lower Mississippi River" (New York: J. H. Colton, 1858); Morgan, "Plat, Field Notes, etc. of Lafayette warrant no. 4, February 11, 1808," Baton Rouge: Louisiana State University.

29. For additional information on the Marquis de Lafayette's visit to Louisiana, see: An Officer in the Late Army, *A Complete History of the Marquis de Lafayette, Major General in the Army of the United States of America, In the War of the Revolution; Embracing an Account of his Late Tour Through the United States to the Time of His Departure, September, 1825* (Hartford, CT: S. Andrus and Son, 1846); Patricia Brady, "Carnival of Liberty: Lafayette in Louisiana," *Louisiana History: The Journal of the Louisiana Historical Association,* XLI (Winter 2000), 23-40; Francis P. Burns, "Lafayette Visits Louisiana," *Louisiana Historical Quarterly* 29 (April 1946), 306; Stanley J. Idzerda, Anne C. Loveland, and Marc H. Miller, *Lafayette, Hero of Two Worlds: The Art and Pageantry of His Farewell Tour of America, 1824-1825* (Flushing, NY: Queens Museum, 1989); Auguste

panied the general on his American tour, never mentions seeing Lafayette's Pointe Coupee land claims.[30] Recent scholarship fails to mention the Pointe Coupée property as well.[31] Legal troubles concerning the exact location of Lafayette's land plagued the general, as well as his descendants. Several Pointe Coupée residents successfully argued that Lafayette's claims were in material conflict with older grants, requiring their relocation. Indeed one case, involving Evariste Blanc and George W. Lafayette, son of the Marquis, proceeded all the way to the United States Supreme Court.[32]

The reverence shown to the Marquis de Lafayette for his part in the American Revolution through the exercise of land warrants in Louisiana held unintended consequences for the U.S. government. The use of federal resources in order to secure the best possible lands for Lafayette, a non-resident, fostered discontent among Louisianans instead of maintaining tranquility at a crucial time in the early U.S. territorial period. Public reaction surrounding the search for available lands and the subsequent litigation concerning Lafayette's Pointe Coupée property exemplified local wariness towards Anglo-American government not unlike the colonists' suspicions of their earlier Spanish administrators. Indeed, the timing of the 1809 Pointe Coupée Census, following the division of the Louisiana Purchase into two districts, amidst Claiborne's and Duplantier's attempts to secure valuable land for Lafayette, and just prior to the United States 1810 Census, indicates a strong local attempt to guarantee that land titles were secure from U.S. attempts to incorporate Louisiana lands into federal public lands jurisdiction. Nevertheless, the namesake communities and monuments of Louisiana, unlike others in the United States, can boast an actual connection to the Marquis. Lafayette owned land among the predominantly francophone Louisianans who also fought the British in the American Revolution under

---

Levasseur, *Lafayette in America in 1824 and 1825; or, Journal of a Voyage to the United States,* trans. John D. Godman, 2 vols. (Philadelphia: Carey and Lea, 1829).

30. Auguste Levasseur, *Lafayette in America in 1824 and 1825; or, Journal of a Voyage to the United States,* trans. John D. Godman, 2 vols. (Philadelphia: Carey and Lea, 1829).

31. Patricia Brady, "Carnival of Liberty: Lafayette in Louisiana," *Louisiana History: The Journal of the Louisiana Historical Association*, 41, no. 1 (Winter, 2000), 23-40; Burns, Francis P., "Lafayette Visits Louisiana," *Louisiana Historical Quarterly*, 29 (1946), 296-340.

32. Stephen K. Williams, ed., *Cases Argued and Decided in the Supreme Court of the United States*, Book 13 (Rochester, NY: The Lawyers' Cooperative Publishing Company, 1901), 104-13.

Bernardo de Galvez. Some of the veterans under Lafayette's command, such as Duplantier, left France and settled in Louisiana following the war. Despite his French heritage, and his service to both the American and French Revolutions, his connections to the Anglo-Americans posed an insurmountable obstacle to the inhabitants of Louisiana allowing the allocation of valuable real estate property on the Isle of Orleans in his name. One wonders, in spite of his many natural connections here, if Lafayette indeed would have felt at home in Louisiana.

7 The Marquis de Lafayette and Lafayette, Louisiana: Identity and Irony

Michael S. Martin

This volume, based on a series of lectures given in Lafayette, Louisiana, to mark the 250th anniversary of the birth of the Marquis de Lafayette, considers the Marquis in French, American, and Atlantic contexts. It addresses a wide variety of issues surrounding the life and legacy of this singular figure in Colonial American history, but it has a special role to play in examining Lafayette's connections and legacy in Louisiana, and the commonalities in the Franco-American experience and history that the Marquis de Lafayette represents and that Louisiana, and in particular Lafayette, Louisiana, embodies. Americans have had a remarkable propensity for naming places after Marie Joseph Paul Yves Roch Gilbert du Motier, the Marquis de Lafayette. Place names are not created on a lark. Much thought usually goes into what to call a particular town, city, county, or parish, and the sheer number of towns named after significant historical actors is a direct reflection not only of those actors' places in the actual history of a nation or state, but also of the way they are remembered.

The fact that this community in south Louisiana, like so many others around the country, chose to honor this figure begs the question: who was this Marquis de Lafayette? How did he get so many places named after him? What were his connections to Louisiana? Born into the nobility in 1757 in Auvergne, France, Lafayette was orphaned by the age of twelve, but, by his late teens, he had married and started a family, entered the brotherhood of Freemasons, and begun a military career. In 1776, he withdrew from the French military and volunteered his services to the fledgling American colonials in their War for Independence from the British. Arriving in Charleston, South Carolina, in 1777, Lafayette trekked to Philadelphia, where the American government granted him the status of major general. He participated in the Battle of Brandywine, spent the horrid winter of 1777 and 1778 at Valley Forge with General Washington, and planned an aborted invasion of Canada. Following the creation of the Franco-American alliance in 1778,

Lafayette departed for France, where he used his connections to lobby for the American cause. He returned to North America in 1780 and, in 1781, when he was only twenty-four-years old, played a critical role in hampering Lord Cornwallis's movements in Virginia, thus buying time for Washington and the Comte de Rochambeau to arrive from New York.

Combining their forces, Washington, Rochambeau, and Lafayette—with aid from a French fleet—encircled Cornwallis at the Battle of Yorktown and, after a relatively brief siege, forced a British surrender in October 1781. Although some minor skirmishing occurred in North America following Yorktown, the British, distracted by concerns elsewhere in the world and cognizant of the fact that the Americans, in tandem with the French, could defeat a highly trained, well-supplied, and professional army of redcoats, gradually capitulated. Negotiations began to end the war and acknowledge American independence. Both of those goals were finalized in the Peace of Paris of 1783.

Lafayette's role in the War for American Independence transcended his on-the-battlefield activities. His participation on the American side had an important validating effect for the patriots. Here was a European nobleman—cultured, wealthy, and otherwise disinterested—fighting on the Americans' side and espousing their ideals. His participation was like a seal of approval for the patriots' fledgling experiment, and his endorsements of their actions and their new nation—which he did repeatedly up until his death—would continue to bolster the Americans' sense that they had taken the correct path.

Lafayette returned to France in late 1781, where, until the onset of his own nation's revolution, he devoted himself to maintaining—and strengthening—the Franco-American alliance. He initially supported and lent his considerable prestige to the French Revolution—first as a member of the National Assembly and then as organizer and commander of the National Guard. By 1792, however, Lafayette had fallen from favor of the Revolution's leaders and was declared a traitor. He subsequently fled to Flanders, where he was captured by the Austrians and placed in prison for five years.

Finally returning to France in 1799, Lafayette refrained from politics during Napoleon's reign and devoted much of his time to scientific farming at his estate, La Grange. He served in the Chamber of Deputies during the late 1810s and early 1820s. In the mid-1820s, Lafayette had made his famous tour of the young United States, and by the late 1820s, he became an increasingly vocal critic of the Bourbon government, a key element of his criticism being the French government's shortcomings when compared to that of the United States. During the Revolution of 1830, Lafayette again took charge of the National Guard, a position from which he might have proclaimed a republic based on the American model. He did not do so, however, and instead threw his support to Louis Phillipe, the Duc D'Orleans, who established a constitutional monarchy. Lafayette died in 1834 and was buried in Picpus cemetery in Paris.

Until the early twentieth-century, most historians writing about Lafayette propagated myths that had developed as early as his own lifetime. Lafayette was seen by these early historians as a supremely virtuous, heroic, and transcendent figure, motivated solely by his good nature and high ideals. Louis Gottschalk, who wrote a magisterial, multivolume biography of Lafayette over the course of the middle decades of the twentieth-century, first began to weed out the myth from the reality. Gottschalk defined, to a large extent, what is known as the ironic nature of Lafayette, that irony being that Lafayette is remembered as the hero of not one, not two, but three revolutions, and yet, when all the facts are considered, his roles in those revolutions really were not all that important compared to those played by others. Indeed, Gottschalk claimed that the irony expanded when one assessed Lafayette's revolutionary motives. Rather than high ideals of liberalism and republicanism, Lafayette, according to Gottschalk, tended to be spurred on by a thirst for fame and adulation.

If Gottschalk is important because he began to dispel the myths of Lafayette, he is also important because he took those myths seriously. Indeed, Gottschalk made the myth part of the story by evaluating not only what Lafayette did and why he did it, but also by assessing how others' opinions of the Marquis influenced their own actions. In a sense, Gottschalk's work was a dual biography: one of Lafayette, the other of perception.

Historians since Gottschalk have continued to grapple with Lafayette's mythology, but they have also broadened their inquiries to address other questions. Notably, historians like Lloyd Kramer, have pondered how a person such as Lafayette, born into the nobility and possessing a great deal of prestige under the old system of government in France, could become a champion of liberalism's individual rights and republicanism's representative form of government. Did he learn these things from Washington and his other American compatriots? Did he pick them up "on the street," so to speak, from the other Americans he encountered? Did he learn these things not in America but instead in France before he crossed the ocean? Did his thoughts on the matter continue to develop even after his time in America?

Historians have also debated whether or not there occurred during the late-eighteenth and early-nineteenth centuries a general revolution that ringed the Atlantic—beginning in the British North American colonies, shifting to France and elsewhere in Europe, and maybe even bouncing back to Latin America. For these historians, Lafayette serves as a model for understanding how, if at all, the American and the other revolutions were connected, and how individuals of the day understood those connections.

Recently, historians such as Kramer, Anne Loveland, and Sandra Frink have keyed in on the notion of "identity" and how Lafayette—and his mythology—fostered the development of a national identity in the United States. Although the debate is contentious, there is some agreement that Lafayette, through his assertions about the benefits of American-style politics and government, was particularly important in helping Americans identify their nation, and themselves, as self-confident and exceptional. Furthermore, through his actions, Lafayette provided a model of sorts, for both the new nation's leaders and its citizenry of what a good American should be and how one should act. This was particularly true during and after his American tour in 1824-25, and it was no less true in Louisiana than elsewhere.

But the situation in Louisiana was different. Louisiana had a distinctive history compared to the other U. S. states. Under first the French and then the Spanish, the colony had been planned, settled, and governed for different reasons and by different kinds of people than the British colonies that stretched from Georgia to Maine. Nor did these differences go away with the stroke of a pen in 1803. Following the Purchase, Louisianans faced an identity crisis, to use a modern term. They lived in what was a territory of the United States, but—because they were mostly Catholic, mostly of non-English descent, and mostly unfamiliar with republican forms of government—they viewed their new national ties with suspicion. And the suspicion was mutual: Many people in the United States viewed their new fellow citizens with wary eyes.

President Thomas Jefferson understood this problem, and he knew that if one person could overcome these difficulties, it was Lafayette. The marquis, after all, was French, but he spoke English; was a member of the nobility, but he had been converted—so to speak—to republicanism; was, because of his French citizenship, considered Catholic, but he was not a practicing one. Jefferson offered to Lafayette the job of territorial governor of Louisiana, but Lafayette turned him down. Ultimately, in what at the time was a controversial appointment (in hindsight it turned out to be a brilliant move), Jefferson appointed William Charles Cole Claiborne to the position.

Having an American of English stock as territorial governor did not solve the dilemma of Louisiana's identity, however, and, even by the time of its admittance as a state in 1812, a great deal of consternation remained both inside and outside of Louisiana as to the state's citizens' ability to function as Americans. The Battle of New Orleans changed that perception somewhat; Louisianans of many different ethnicities worked together with regular American soldiers and their leader Andrew Jackson to defeat an army of British regulars. The battle showed that Louisianans were willing to fight, and in a few instances, die, for their new nation. But doubts still lingered on both sides: non-Louisianans considered the state an anomaly and a potential problem. Louisianans understood how others perceived them and their state, and many felt unaccepted, even unwelcome, as part of the United States.

Lafayette's visit in 1825 played a remarkable role in shifting the way Louisianans defined themselves. On Sunday, April 10, at the battlefield in Chalmette, the marquis disembarked from the steamboat *Natchez*, which he had taken from Mobile, Alabama. He then traveled overland into New Orleans. There, he dwelled at the Cabildo, the city hall, which had been redecorated and, to an extent, remodeled specifically for his visit. For a week, Lafayette visited with city and state dignitaries, received guests, attended dinners, plays, balls, and concerts, and reviewed local militia units. Although he made no formal speeches, Lafayette's sheer presence in the city made a lasting impression on both New Orleans and Louisiana.

Lafayette's visit solidified identity among Louisianans. In much the same way his participation in the War for American Independence seemed to validate for Americans the correctness of their cause, for Louisianans, his visit confirmed their status as Americans. Lafayette's stopover in the Crescent City elevated it to the level of other great American cities he visited, and his dual image as both hero of the American Revolution and noble Frenchman made it easier for Louisianans to portray themselves as both patriotic and good Americans yet also descendents of non-English settlers.

In honor of Lafayette's visit, the city of New Orleans named a street and a square after him. Just upriver, encompassing a portion of what is today's Garden District, the former plantation lands of John Poultney were subdivided into Faubourg Lafayette. In 1833, Faubourg Lafayette was combined with two other subdivisions, incorporated, and deemed the City of Lafayette. The city existed until 1852, when it was annexed by New Orleans.

Which raises the question of the name of present-day Lafayette, Louisiana. How did Lafayette Parish and the city of Lafayette come to be so named?

Not too many years before the marquis ventured to North America to aid the Americans in their battles against the British, Europeans made their first visits to a spot on the Vermilion River that they initially called Petit Manchac. This would have been at or very near to the present site of the

Pinhook Road Bridge over the Vermilion River in present-day Lafayette. Over the years, a settlement sprang up in the area, the name changed to Pin Hook (no one is really sure where the term comes from), then simply Vermilion (sometimes St. Jean au Vermilion) and finally, by the early nineteenth century, Vermilionville.

In 1823, the Louisiana state legislature carved Lafayette Parish, named in the Marquis' honor, from St. Martin Parish. Jean Mouton, a local plantation owner and land speculator, then offered to donate land near a small Catholic chapel on the far end of his plantation for a courthouse site; after a hotly disputed campaign, the voters of the Parish agreed to that site for their new parish seat. Thus the center of population shifted away from the banks of the Vermilion to what is now considered downtown.

The courthouse and church drew residences and shops to their area, and, as a result of the hamlet's growth, in 1836, the legislature incorporated the town of Vermilionville. Town leaders had wanted the place to be renamed Lafayette, both to honor the Marquis, who had only recently died, and to match up with the Parish's name. But that name had been granted to the New Orleans suburb only three years before. It would be nearly five decades before Vermilionville became Lafayette in 1884. Obviously, the name has stuck.

And, of course, the name is important. If the Marquis de Lafayette had become an identifying symbol for Americans both inside and outside of Louisiana, what better announcement of that identification than by taking his name itself. The state legislature obviously had in mind honoring the hero when it named the new parish after him in 1823, but what is more remarkable is the significance of that name more than sixty years later, when both city leaders and state legislators agreed to change Vermilionville's name to Lafayette.

Besides a common name, the Marquis de Lafayette and the parish/city of Lafayette have some other commonalities. First, it is obvious that both the Marquis and our area have been, at times, misunderstood and criticized by their own nations. During his lifetime, Lafayette's image in the minds of Frenchmen waxed and waned as revolutions begat stability and then new revolutions. At times he was viewed as a hero, at others a scapegoat; at times he was deemed too radical, at others too conservative.

Lafayette Parish and its citizens, too; indeed all of Acadiana and even all of south Louisiana, have faced similar shifts in the opinions of outsiders. For much of their history, the people of Lafayette and surrounding areas have been viewed as odd, different, even un-American. Outsiders noted that they ate strange food and danced to exotic music. They lived in curious locations and they worked at strange labors. Worst of all, they were not Protestants and they spoke no English. For someone from the North or the West, or even from other areas of the South, the people and culture of this Lafayette and its environs were bizarre, perhaps mysterious but more often simply un-American. Up until well after World War II, the image most Americans had of south Louisiana was decidedly negative.

But like the Marquis' image, Lafayette and south Louisiana's has been rehabilitated, thanks largely to just some of those distinctive characteristics earlier outsiders found so strange. The exportation, and exploitation, of Cajun and Creole music and cuisine elsewhere in the nation has led to rather positive assessments of the area by other Americans, although certainly many cling to the sense that people from here are somehow fundamentally different from those elsewhere.

The second theme relating Lafayette the man to Lafayette the community has to do with the sense of the Marquis being "a hero of two worlds." Lafayette prides itself on being an internationally connected place, particularly within the francophone world. It maintains cultural connections with French-speaking areas of Canada, the Caribbean, Asia, Africa, and, of course, with France itself. Particularly since the late 1960s, the city's leaders and many of its citizens have strengthened those connections while forging new ones. If the Marquis de Lafayette was a "hero of two worlds"—the old and the new—then we might rightly say that Lafayette, Louisiana, is a community of "two worlds."

But there is more to it than this. I mentioned above that historian Louis Gottschalk first pointed out that Lafayette's story was particularly ironic. The irony was that, although he is considered "the hero of two worlds," the Marquis in reality was not particularly heroic on either side of the Atlantic. And there is an irony in the way Lafayette might be defined as a community "of two worlds." That irony is this: By defining itself in terms of its francophone connections, Lafayette is potentially ignoring other worlds to which it is connected.

If we look really closely, we will find that Lafayette is a community of many worlds. Even among the French speakers in the area, divisions exist. There are people who, whether because of their family backgrounds or their own personal proclivities, speak Cajun French, Creole French, continental French, or some combination of them all. In fact, heated disputes have arisen between those espousing one form of French over another. Aside from the francophone cultures, however, there exist here numerous other cultures that might be defined by language—English and Spanish speakers, for instance—or other ethnic or cultural backgrounds. Because of their situation in Lafayette, those groups are often marginalized by Lafayette's cultural promoters, who thus present to outsiders a skewed perspective of what this place is really like.

Of course, the greatest irony is that, even decades after attempts to create a renaissance of French-speaking in the area, most citizens of Lafayette speak very little French or none at all. English has become the dominant language. Many of these English speakers are descendants of French speakers whose families have lived here for generations, but, somewhere along the line gave up the language of their ancestors. Other English speakers are relative newcomers who arrived some time in the last century.

But the basic fact is that people in Lafayette, whatever their ancestry, are very much more like other Americans than they are like other non-Americans. And here is the final irony: in a time when Lafayette prides itself on being different as a way of attracting tourists, it has become much like the places those outsiders leave behind to come here. They have malls; we have malls. They have suburbs; we have suburbs. They have fast food chains; we have fast food chains. Where once the Marquis de Lafayette provided a symbolic identifier for Americans everywhere—including here—today such an identifier is largely unnecessary. Americans here and elsewhere identify with one another because they really are similar.

8 Integrity V. Hypocrisy: Lafayette and Race in the Revolutionary Atlantic

Bradley Pollock

> . . . your celebration is a sham; your boasted liberty, an unholy license; your national greatness, swelling vanity, your sounds of rejoicing are empty and heartless, your denunciation of tyrants, brass fronted impudence; your shouts of liberty and equality, hollow mockery; your prayers and hymns, your sermons and thanksgivings, . . . are to him mere bombast, fraud, deception, impiety and hypocrisy—a thin veil to cover up crimes that would disgrace a nation of savages. There is not a nation on the earth guilty of practices, more shocking and bloody, than are the people of these United States, at this very hour.
>
> Go where you may, search where you will, roam through all the monarchies and despotisms of the old world, travel through South America, search out every abuse and when you have found the last, lay your facts by the side of the every day practices of this nation, and you will say with me, that, for revolting barbarity and shameless hypocrisy, America reigns without a rival.[1]

Although this passage from Frederick Douglass' famous "Fourth of July Oration" was first uttered nearly seven decades after the Marquis de Lafayette's efforts to abolish slavery, it reflects the central issue in Lafayette's abolitionism as well as many of the essential contradictions in American culture, conscience, and politics.

In the age of the American and French Revolutions, two generations before Douglass himself became an abolitionist, a great debate was raging on both sides of the Atlantic. Societies and groups that claimed to believe in the "natural rights of men" were enslaving Africans by the millions and had

1. Frederick Douglass, "What, to the Slave, is the Fourth of July," in *Lift Every Voice: African American Oratory, 1787-1900*, eds. Philip S. Foner and Robert J. Iranham (Tuscaloosa: University of Alabama Press, 1998), 258.

conducted a slave trade for roughly three centuries that had killed millions more. Among American Revolutionaries, men like James Otis, Thomas Paine, and Benjamin Franklin stood out as outspoken critics of this peculiar institution. According to Thomas Paine:

> Our Traders in MEN (an unnatural commodity?) must know the wickedness of the SLAVE TRADE, if they attend to reasoning, or the dictates of Their own hearts: and such as shun and stifle all these, willfully sacrifice Conscience, and the character of integrity to that golden idol.[2]

The fact that their criticism "stood out" seems itself peculiar if one considers that the ideals of "natural rights philosophy" were supposed to be the ideological heart of this revolution. If according to John Locke the purpose of government was to protect human life, liberty and property or, as Jefferson would coin and a contemporary motion picture title would today echo, "the pursuit of happiness," then revolutionary leaders like George Washington and Thomas Jefferson who were also major slaveholders, were hypocrites indeed. African slaves were allowed no right to their own life or control of their destiny. Slaves not only had no property rights that slaveholders could not violate at will, they were themselves considered "chattel property." Slavery in its essence is a complete denial of liberty and although a slave might "pursue happiness" by seeking freedom, white society in general and elite slaveholders in particular had marshaled the resources and power of an entire society, with its economic, political, social, and cultural forces, to crush that pursuit in any possible form, down to the level of the psyche, down to the level of the dream of freedom.

Nevertheless, another set of ideas was just as basic to American society as "natural rights," and more fundamental to Western civilization as a whole, and that was the doctrine and worldview of white supremacy. By the late 1700s racism and notions of white supremacy were part of the fabric of all the societies involved in the slave trade and beyond. Greed, racism, and a desire to maintain white power and domination were, in fact, far more important to slave holders and to whites in general than high humanitarian ideals or notions of "natural rights." This contradiction is clear and plain and has been at the heart of the American psyche since the birth of the nation.

The Marquis de Lafayette was a man of his time and had been raised and trained in a white supremacist milieu; that is why his stand against slav-

2. Thomas Paine, "African Slavery in America," *The Pennsylvania Journal and the Weekly Advertiser*, March 8, 1775.

ery highlights his own integrity. Friends and associates of his like Thomas Jefferson and George Washington would continue to claim devotion to natural rights ideals and yet maintain their own slave ownership and support of slavery. At one point in his life Washington was the country's largest slaveholder, and at the beginning of the Revolution he was very much against the enlistment of blacks in the Continental Army. Washington did not want to promise freedom to slaves who fought in support of the Revolution. He did not even favor the idea of arming and training free blacks. Ignoring natural rights ideals, Washington did not intend that winning independence from England would have any impact on slavery at all. It was only when Lord Murray Dunmore offered freedom to slaves who fought for the British that Washington was compelled to make a similar offer. The alternative was to risk the entire black community supporting the British as a path to freedom. Even so, slaveholders had the final decision: Washington saw to it that no slaveholder had to allow his slaves to enlist. It was voluntary; often slaves who were allowed to enlist took the place of their master or their masters' oldest son. In fact, most slaves who fought in the Revolution were fugitive slaves who had escaped from slavery and fought in the Revolution to legitimize their free status. Dunmore's offer became British policy in 1776 but the Continental Congress did not order the active recruitment of black troops, slave or free, until the spring of 1779. Although Washington would decide to free his own slaves at the end of his life, he did not equate the ideals of the Revolution with the destruction of slavery as an institution.

Thomas Jefferson was perhaps more uneasy than Washington with the notion of fighting a war for freedom while maintaining a system of slavery. Jefferson would often go to great lengths to rationalize the continuance of slavery while being aware that that very continuance was a moral condemnation of his nation and a threat to its future. In a letter to Lafayette in reference to the Compromise of 1820, Jefferson wrote:

> All know that permitting the slaves of the South to spread into the West will not add one being to that unfortunate condition, that it will increase the happiness of those existing, and by spreading them over a larger surface, will dilute the evil everywhere, and facilitate the means of getting finally rid of it, an event more anxiously wished by those on whom it presses than by the noisy pretenders to exclusive humanity.[3]

3. Thomas Jefferson to M. de la Fayette, December 26, 1820, in *The Writings of Thomas Jefferson; Being His Autobiograph, Correspondence, Reports, Messages, Adddresses, and Other Writings, Official and Private,* vol. VII, ed. H. A. Washington, (Washington,

Jefferson clearly thinks the nation will be better off when slavery is gone, yet he promotes its spread, claiming that this will hasten its ending. Lafayette, on the other hand, was a consistent abolitionist from early adulthood to the end of his life. He attempted, through his association with American leaders, to push forward the agenda of emancipation. Even so, his is a mild and moderate abolitionism. Lafayette's criticism is aimed at highlighting the contradictions between republicanism and slavery, in hopes that men like Jefferson who were aware of the contradictions would act from integrity rather than prejudice and personal interest. Lafayette does not wield the fiery words of a William Lloyd Garrison and he is not the hero of the cause of the slave that many would later find in John Brown or even more in Harriet Tubman or Frederick Douglass. On the other hand, Lafayette does attempt to be a spark of conscience for men like Jefferson. Responding to the letter noted above, Lafayette writes:

> ... I would have thought that by spreading the prejudices, habits and calculation of planters over a larger surface you rather increase the difficulties of final liberation. Was it not for that deplorable circumstance of negro slavery in the Southern States not a word could be objected, when we present American doctrines and constitutions as an example to Old Europe?[4]

Lafayette was influenced by Quaker critiques of slavery that reflected the ideas of men like Dr. Benjamin Rush, who noted that slaveholders' mass conversion of African slaves to Christianity proved white awareness of African humanity and made the continued enslavement of Africans illogical, immoral, hypocritical, and evil. Even more important was the influence on Lafayette by the work of men like Granville Sharp and Thomas Clarkson of the British abolition movement, as well as the French Abolitionist Marquis de Condorcet.[5]

In terms of the American abolitionist tradition, it can be argued that Lafayette's approach and temper was far from that of Levi Coffin or John Fairfield of Underground Railroad fame but closer to that of moderate abolitionists like Theodore Weld or the Tappan brothers. Weld and other moderate abolitionists of the antebellum period sought compensation by government

---

D.C.: Taylor & Maury, 1854), 194.

4. Lafayette to Jefferson, July 1, 1821, in *The Letters of Lafayette and Jefferson*, ed. Gilbert Chinard, (Baltimore: The Johns Hopkins Press, 1929), 407.

5. See Melvin D. Kennedy, *Lafayette and Slavery: From His Letters to Thomas Clarkson and Granville Sharp* (Baltimore: J. H. Furst Co., 1950).

for slaveholders who voluntarily emancipated their slaves. This kind of abolitionism has among its roots the work of eighteenth-century abolitionists like Lafayette, whose focus was more on the incongruence of slavery and republicanism and the issue of the conscience of white society, than it was on the actual fate and lives of blacks.

Yet, as many have said of his friend Thomas Jefferson, Lafayette was a complex man, for unlike most abolitionists of his day Lafayette critiqued racism itself as well as slavery. He wrote to John Adams in 1786:

> In the cause of my black brethren I feel myself warmly interested, and most decidedly side, so far as respects them, against the white part of mankind. Whatever be the complexion of the enslaved, it does not, in my opinion, alter the complexion of the crime which the enslaver commits—a crime much blacker than any African face.[6]

Relative to the racist milieu of the time this is a rather odd statement. Some would claim that this attitude on the part of Lafayette was due to his friendship with James Armistead. Armistead served with Lafayette in the American Revolution, during the Richmond siege in 1781. Armistead would later work behind British lines as a spy, helping to make possible the American victory at Yorktown. Later in 1787 Lafayette wrote a testimonial on Armistead's behalf that helped him win his freedom through the Virginia General Assembly. Perhaps close association with Armistead made Lafayette aware that Armistead was in no way inferior to other men and far braver than many white men. This may indeed have created a more open attitude in Lafayette on the issue of race than most white men of his time, including most abolitionists. It is worth noting that Jefferson formed an association with Benjamin Baneker, commissioning him to work on parts of the design of the new capitol in Washington, D.C. It was Jefferson who also sent a copy of one of Baneker's almanacs to the French Academy of Sciences to consider for publication in France. According to many scholars, Baneker was a genius, a student of the enlightenment, a scientist and engineer, astronomer and inventor, a great man of letters, and an international peace activist. Yet Jefferson remained ambivalent on the issue of black inferiority, and would not be moved to call for a quick end to slavery or even the emancipation of his own slaves, some of whom he formed very close associations with as

6. Lafayette to John Adams, February 22, 1786, quoted in *Encyclopedia of African American History, 1619-1815, From the Colonial Period to the Age of Frederick Douglas*, vol. 2, Paul Finkelman, ed. in chief (New York: Oxford University Press, 2006), 246.

well.

During the late eighteenth century there were many other examples of blacks achieving intellectual accomplishment and fundamental individual equality, as well as awareness of their power to do so. Poets such as Lucy Terry, entrepreneurs like Paul Cuffe and James Derharm, a medical doctor and ex-slave . . . the list is legion but perhaps most relevant to this discussion at this point, was a petition to Connecticut's General Assembly submitted by two slaves on behalf of themselves and other Africans throughout the state that embodies the espoused ideology of revolutionaries like Jefferson with more clarity and less contradiction than Jefferson himself.

> Reason and Revelation join to declare that we are the creatures of that God, who made of one Blood, and kindred, all the nations of the Earth; we perceive by our own reflection, that we are endowed with the same faculties with our masters, and there is nothing that leads us to a belief, or suspicion, that we are any more obliged to serve them, than they us, and the more we consider of this matter, the more we are convinced of our right . . . to be free . . . and can never be convinced that we were made to be slaves . . . we do ask for nothing, but what we are fully persuaded is ours to claim.[7]

The comparison between Jefferson and Lafayette is a useful one. Not only were they friends but both were men of letters and considered themselves committed to republican ideals. It was Lafayette's desire to live according to those ideals that motivated and informed his abolitionism and sustained his integrity, while Jefferson's inability to live up to his ideals undermined his integrity and led him into hypocrisy. This same hypocrisy allowed white American politicians to repeatedly compromise on the issue of slavery, valuing white unity over justice, from Article I of the Constitution through the three-fifths compromise, the Missouri Compromise, the Compromise of 1850, and others. It was that same hypocrisy that allowed many Americans to turn a blind eye to lynching and other forms of racial violence and intimidation. It was that same hypocrisy that during the Jim Crow era allowed the government to send black men to fight and die for the United States when the same nation would not fight for them. As recently as the 1960s, black soldiers could not vote in their home states and the government would not protect them from domestic terrorists. The same hypocrisy fuels

7. "Petition of 1779 by slaves of Fairfield County for the abolition of Slavery in Connecticut," in *A Documentary History of the Negro People in the United States,* vol. 1, ed. Herbert Aptheker, (New York: Citadel Press, 1951), 10-12.

America's race problems down to the present day. It is the same hypocrisy that even today causes many Americans to rationalize "racial profiling" or justify police brutality against blacks.

* * *

The United States, both historically and at present, is a multi-cultural, multi-racial, highly diverse society. If we accept that what has held it together so far are shared beliefs in a basic set of principles, we must be clear on what constitutes these core values. These core values are rooted in the ideology of the American Revolution. Among these principles are: individual rights, government by consent of the governed, civil liberties (i.e., freedom of speech, press, religion, thought and assembly), equality under the law, and equal opportunity (as well as the socio-economic mobility that such a concept necessitates). Nevertheless, it is the abstract belief in these principles, not their manifested reality, that has created America's core identity. These are the key elements of the political culture that defines America. However, a deep devotion to an ideology of white supremacy is also a firm and contradictory part of that national cultural identity. The schism and divisions that we experience in America today are not a result of the promotion of diversity, multi-cultural movements or pluralism, or freedom of thought. These forces are not disuniting America, breaking up something that was once unified. It is rather a long tradition of duplicity in American culture and politics that is the greatest threat to a true American unity. The menace is a heritage of hypocrisy and counter-intention that begins with belief in "The Rights of Man" being professed by slaveholders and ends with recent popular attempts to justify the beating and killing of innocent blacks. This hypocrisy, this sinister duplicity that has racism as its taproot, is older than the nation itself.

The Marquis de Lafayette was not a champion of African freedom per se. He was more concerned about the future of white America than the future of blacks. He was more worried about the souls of whites than the liberty and equality of Africans. Nevertheless, Lafayette saw this American hypocrisy clearly. He encouraged others to face its reality and he consistently made a personal effort not to give in to its cultural gravity. How many Americans, past or present can say the same?

CPSIA information can be obtained
at www.ICGtesting.com
Printed in the USA
LVOW12s2030120716
495415LV00002B/2/P

9 781935 754671